Richard Beatty's

JOB SEARCH
NETWORKING

Richard Beatty's

JOB SEARCH NETWORKING

BOB ADAMS, INC.
Holbrook, Massachusetts

Published by Bob Adams, Inc.
260 Center Street, Holbrook, MA 02343

ISBN: 1-55850-402-8

Printed in the United States of America.

J I H G F E D C B

Library of Congress Cataloging-in-Publication Data
Beatty, Richard H., 1939-
    [Job search networking]
    Richard Beatty's Job search networking.
    p.   cm.
    Includes index.
    ISBN 1-55850-402-8
    1. Job hunting. 2. Social networks. I. Title.
HF5382.7.B443   1994
650.14—dc20   94-28765
                                                        CIP

This publication is designed to provide accurate and authoritative information with regard to the subject matter covered. It is sold with the understanding that the publisher is not engaged in rendering
legal, accounting, or other professional advice. If legal advice or other expert assistance is required, the
services of a competent professional person should be sought.
    — From a *Declaration of Principles* jointly adopted by a Committee of the American Bar Association
                                                    and a Committee of Publishers and Associations

This book is available at quantity discounts for bulk purchases.
For information, call 1-800-872-5627.

To those who dare to dream and soar
far above the deafening crowd
and reach out for the vision of
a better day.

Contents

Introduction

In survey after survey, employment networking has been long been cited as the *predominant source* by which jobs are found. Most surveys that have studied how white collar workers find employment, in fact, estimate that between 64 percent and 75 percent of all jobs are found using networking or personal contact. In addition, these same studies consistently show that employment networking accounts for between *two to three times more jobs than all other employment sources combined*—a rather impressive statistic!

Despite its unquestioned preeminence as a job-hunting tool, until now there has never been a book published solely on the topic of employment networking. This is quite amazing, considering millions of unemployed Americans have been struggling to find employment, with practically nowhere to turn to learn the effective networking skills so critical to job-hunting success. Fortunately, this book will take job hunters by the hand and arm them with the essential tools of the networking trade.

A few years back, I spent three years working as a vice president and consultant for one of America's largest human resources consulting firms. I was employed as a senior consultant in the firm's executive search division, and was handling senior level search assignments for several large billion-dollar international clients. Interestingly, this consulting firm was in the outplacement consulting business as well, and the executive search practice was located on the same floor as the outplacement consulting practice, but at opposite ends of the building.

Since I was writing books on job search at the time, I would often spend my coffee breaks talking with several of the firm's clients, who had recently been separated from their employers and were going through the consulting firm's outplacement program. Since many of these individuals were aware of my status as a job-hunting author, as well as my experience in the field of executive search consulting, they frequently asked my advice on job-hunting strategies and techniques, which I freely volunteered.

During my frequent daily treks to the "outplacement consulting wing," I began to witness firsthand the pain that many of these men and women were going through in their attempts to effectively network. In my judgment the consulting firm was not doing a very good job providing "skills" training in networking techniques. Instead, most of the training in networking was "conceptual" in nature—program participants were being trained in the concepts and theory of networking, but weren't receiving practical, how-to advice for doing it well. The firm was, however, promoting networking as *the* way to find employment.

The consequences of this inadequate training, coupled with the firm's emphasis on networking as the primary vehicle for finding employment, was causing a lot of frustration and anxiety. In fact, I could quickly spot those who were in about the fifth or sixth week of their job search on the basis of their facial expressions alone. It was clear that many, at this stage of their job search, were experiencing a state of depression.

What was actually going on was that these individuals had worked very hard at networking for the first month or so of their job search and "nothing had happened." They had, in fact, exhausted their first level of networking contacts (those whom they knew personally) and were having little or no success developing the job leads or new contacts that are so critical to keeping the networking process alive.

This lack of success was devastating to egos that had already been badly bruised during the employment separation process, and now they were suffering a further assault on their sense of value and self-image. At this stage they had begun to turn inward, and question their self-worth. After all, they were making a strong effort to find employment, but market feedback suggested they "weren't worth anything."

Unfortunately, many of these individuals were very talented, capable, proud people and, on the basis of their solid past performance and contributions, did not deserve to feel this way about themselves. The real culprit, in my judgment, was not their "market worth" but, instead, the "lack of adequate training" in practical, usable and effective networking techniques. To put it bluntly, they were enduring a lot of unwarranted psychological pain and anguish that might have been avoided had they been given better training in specific networking strategies and techniques.

Employment separation can be a devastating experience for anyone going through it, and I couldn't help but feel a great deal of empathy for the enormous emotional turmoil that many of these talented professionals were experiencing. As a result, I made the personal commitment that I was going to find better ways to do networking that would alleviate much of the anxiety and suffering so frequently associated with the networking process. (This, by the way, became the principal motivation for writing this book.)

During my frequent informal meetings with these outplacement program participants, I began to offer ideas and suggestions for improving their networking skills, and asked my newfound test group to provide me with feedback on how well these recommendations worked. Specifically, I was looking for ways to help them shortcut the networking process and make them more effective at achieving successful networking results. Much of my learning from this (and subsequent) experimentation with networking strategies and techniques are contained in this book.

Job Search Networking is designed to be a comprehensive how-to book on employment networking. The book's contents are presented in a logical, step-by-step how-to sequence that is designed to facilitate learning of the entire employment networking process, from the planning phase through actual application. It not only provides an understanding of broad networking concepts, but also presents the equivalent of a thorough training course that will help you to become a proficient networker. The emphasis is heavily on skills training, in other words, the specific "how to do it" techniques that are essential to becoming a good networker.

This essential guide is also chock full of numerous specific examples showing how the strategies and techniques can actually be applied. These same examples also serve as models you can use to develop your own personally tailored versions of these networking techniques.

The first three chapters deal with the employment networking concept—what networking is and how it works. Various studies are also cited to emphasize the extreme importance of networking as the most powerful of job hunting techniques. Very thorough chapters are then presented on the critical topics of planning the networking process, making networking telephone calls, and conducting productive networking meetings. Other chapters cover such important topics as getting past the secretary/gatekeeper, overcoming common networking barriers, developing successful networking strategies, and networking tricks and shortcuts that can cut valuable time off of the job-hunting process.

I believe you will find this book to be a very practical and useful guide in learning how to become proficient at employment networking. Its methodical, step-by-step process approach, combined with numerous practical examples of specific networking techniques, should take much of the mystery and guesswork out of the employment networking process, and provide you with the skills for networking success.

Happy networking!

—RICHARD H. BEATTY
West Chester, PA

Chapter 1

The Case for Employment Networking

Over the years the case for employment networking as the premiere source for successful job hunting has been made rather emphatically. Studies clearly show that this technique, above all others, has time-after-time accounted for more job offers and successful employment searches than all other employment sources combined. And yet, until this book, there has been no book written that solely addresses this area of vital importance to the job seeker.

Hundreds of articles have been published talking about the importance of employment networking as *the* job-hunting methodology; however, most have barely scratched the surface and offer only a brief glimpse of how to do it. Unfortunately, most of what has been written is painfully shallow and does not provide sufficient detail to allow the job hunter to become proficient in the process and skills required for effective networking.

In essence, the importance of networking as a job-hunting tool rests in the fact that networking is the key vehicle by which the job hunter can gain access to the "hidden job market." The term hidden job market means those employment opportunities that have not yet become known to the general public through such communication channels as newspaper classified ads (otherwise known as the "want ads"), employment agencies, executive search firms, the state employment service, etc. In this sense, the jobs remain "hidden" from the public and are known to exist by only a small handful of company employees (typically the hiring manager, his or her department manager, and the manager of human resources).

Getting to these jobs before they are released to the general public places you at a distinct competitive advantage over the masses of qualified candidates with whom you would otherwise need to compete. In fact, if (through effective networking) you can create interest in your employment candidacy before the company takes action to make the job opening known to others, you can literally reduce the competition to zero and end up with a viable employment offer.

Networking, then, becomes the key to conducting an effective job-hunting campaign. Without it, you can render your job search impotent and relegate yourself to only one in a sea of qualified candidates who must compete for the job—one in a cast of thousands, so to speak. With it, you suddenly cast yourself in a far more powerful role and enhance your ability to positively control your career destiny through the virtual elimination of competition.

Critical Voices of Networking

During the last couple of years, I have mused at the growing number of articles appearing in some of the nation's leading newspapers, magazines, and professional journals that have proclaimed, "Networking is dead!" These articles frequently describe, in painstaking detail, the ordeals of job seekers who are frustrated in their attempts to successfully use employment networking as a key element in their quest for employment.

Often, such articles also cite the alleged aversion felt by busy executives who are the recipients of these so-called "nuisance calls" from the unemployed. The general theme is that America's managers have been "networked to death," and have now taken firm steps to assure that these unwanted calls will be intercepted and screened out well in advance. Hence, the conclusion—networking is dead." But, is it really?

Unfortunately, in my judgment, such irresponsible journalism does a great injustice to the job seeker by distorting and obscuring the significance of networking as a major job-hunting source. These articles are extremely misleading and invariably represent the views of only a handful of individuals interviewed by the authors, who have become frustrated with the employment networking process. This is the "man bites dog" phenomenon, and is designed to sell publications (by stirring up controversy) rather than present a well-researched, balanced, and responsible overview of the real world as supported by market facts.

Granted, employment networking does not come easily to most job seekers, and it therefore requires little or no effort for journalists to find those who would be quick to dismiss it as a key job-hunting source. Generally, however, you will find that these are the minority views of those who are still unemployed and have not yet experienced job-hunting success. With such people the frustration associated with networking can understandably run very high. But, for those who have successfully concluded their job search, there is likely to be a much different viewpoint.

What are successful job seekers likely to say about the effectiveness and importance of networking as a job-hunting tool? Studies that show how successful job seekers have actually found their jobs suggest a far more favorable view of employment networking as a principal job-hunting source.

Networking Is Alive and Well in America

Despite what you may hear to the contrary, networking is still very much alive and well in America! Studies of recently employed individuals continue to show that employment networking remains (by far) the number one employment source for both finding and landing jobs. In fact, as an employment technique, networking has been proven to be *two to three times* more productive than all other employment sources *combined*, accounting for an estimated 64 percent to 75 percent of all jobs landed by the job seeker. Some sources, in fact, place this estimate as high as 80 percent!

In order to gain a fuller appreciation for the real importance of networking to job-hunting success, and to further dispel any remaining doubt that may exist in your mind about the importance of networking, let's briefly review some of the key studies that show how jobs are actually found.

The Granovetter Study

A study conducted by Harvard University sociologist Mark S. Granovetter provides substantial proof of the relative importance of networking as a key method for landing employment. This study, published by Harvard University Press and entitled *Getting a Job: a Study of Contacts and Careers*, surveyed several hundred professional, technical and managerial workers and asked them how they had recently found employment. Essentially, Granovetter's findings were as follows:

Percentage of Jobs Found	Employment Source Used
74.5%	Networking
9.9%	Advertising
8.9%	Employment agencies
6.7%	Other sources

Personal contact, or networking, accounted for a full 74.5 percent of all jobs found by the job seekers that Granovetter studied. Stated differently, personal contact accounted for over seven and a half times the results of the next most effective job-hunting source. In fact, according to Granovetter's data, networking has proven to be nearly three times more effective than all other employment sources combined!

Granovetter's study also reveals two other interesting findings that should be of considerable interest to those engaged in a search for employment. These findings are as follow:

- Of those finding employment through networking, some 43.5 percent landed jobs that were newly created to accommodate them.

- The best jobs (those providing highest pay, most prestige, and greatest satisfaction) were found through networking.

So, Granovetter's study provides a very strong case for the importance of employment networking. The power of networking to actually generate or create jobs cannot be overlooked by the conscientious job seeker, particularly in a tight labor market where employment opportunities are few and competition is intense.

U.S. Department of Labor Study

A huge study conducted by the U.S. Department of Labor provides additional credence to Granovetter's findings. This study, termed *Job Seeking Methods Used by American Workers*, covered some 10.4 million men and women who had found jobs. Unlike Granovetter's study, which focused on white collar workers, this study included all categories of hourly wage and salaried workers (excluding farm workers) from professionals and administrators to construction workers and mechanics.

Results of this study were as follow:

Percentage of Jobs Found	Employment Source Used
63.4%	Networking
13.9%	Advertising
12.2%	Employment agencies
10.5%	Other sources

Although networking still remains the most significant factor by far in successful job hunting methodology, there is a drop of a little over 11 percent (63.4 percent versus 74.5 percent) when the Labor Department's findings are compared with those of Granovetter's. I believe the difference in findings is probably attributable to the composition of the groups studied. White collar workers are simply more comfortable and adept at employment networking than their blue collar counterparts, which most likely accounts for the higher networking result in the Granovetter study.

Regardless of the difference in actual percentages of these two studies, it is important to once again recognize the significant role that networking plays in job- hunting results. The U.S. Department of Labor study again confirms that networking is several times more effective at finding employment than any of the other employment sources from which the job seeker might choose. Certainly, 63.4 percent is nothing to sneeze at!

The Brandywine Study

A few years ago my firm, Brandywine Consulting Group, undertook an independent study to further explore how jobs are found. Although certainly not as scientific and statistically pure as the other two studies just cited, the Brandywine study seems to lend further support to the findings of both the Granovetter and U.S. Department of Labor studies as far as the importance of employment networking is concerned.

In the Brandywine study, we surveyed nine of the nation's largest outplacement consulting firms to determine how persons going through their career transition programs were successful in finding employment. Specifically, we were interested in learning which employment sources proved most effective in finding jobs. The firms surveyed included the following:

1. Challenger, Gray & Christmas
2. Drake Beam Morin

3. Executive Assets

4. Jannotta Bray & Associates

5. King, Chapman, Broussard & Gallagher

6. Lee Hecht Harrison

7. Manchester, Inc.

8. Mainstream Access

9. Right Associates

Each of these firms have trained and coached literally thousands of individuals, who have experienced involuntary employment separation in job-hunting methodology and provided consulting support to them throughout the job-hunting process. These firms were selected due to the large numbers of laid-off workers who had been through their job search/career transition programs. Each firm was asked the percentage of jobs their clients found by using the following employment sources:

1. Networking

2. Search firms and employment agencies

3. Recruitment advertising

4. Other sources

Although we were unable to determine the exact number of job seekers covered by this survey, a conservative estimate greatly exceeds 20,000 workers. Thus, due to the size of this study, it is more than likely a reliable indicator of how jobs are found in today's marketplace.

The findings of this Brandywine study were as follows:

Percentage of Jobs Found	Employment Source Used
68%	Networking
14%	Search firms and employment agencies
10%	Recruitment advertising
8%	Other sources

Once again, networking was the overwhelming winner! Accounting for 68 percent of all positions found by workers, networking was nearly five times as effective as the second most productive job-hunting source. And, in fact, it proved to be over two times as productive as *all* other employment sources combined.

Abuses and Misuses of Networking

I believe that many of the unfavorable articles that have been critical of networking are less a matter of statistics and more a matter of networking technique. The statistics clearly establish networking as the most important of all job-hunting sources. Yet, despite the overwhelming statistical evidence, networking still occasionally gets a bad name on the part of job seekers and employers alike.

When negative articles about networking appear in print, I am immediately suspect of the source. From the professional side, I am convinced that the issue is not really the networking process per se, but instead the abuse and misuse of this process by less than adequately-trained job seekers attempting to employ it. If done improperly, networking will, no doubt, prove to be exhausting, frustrating, and highly ineffective. If properly planned and executed by well-trained individuals, however, employment networking will more than prove its metal—time and time again!

When improperly trained, networkers invariably lack the skills essential to getting their contacts to "open up" and to share the kinds of information and/or contacts truly important to job-hunting success. This lack of success quickly becomes discouraging, and networkers are apt to lay the blame on the process rather than themselves. In such cases they are prone to abandon networking early in their job search in favor of easier to use (and far less productive) employment sources. The consequences can be a substantially protracted job search and an unwarranted "black eye" to the reputation of networking as a key job-hunting tool.

Likewise, key networking contacts, when approached by the poorly trained networker, are apt to have a negative reaction to the networking process. When the networker is awkward, too direct, blunt, disorganized, or otherwise clumsy in his or her networking approach, these important contacts can readily become annoyed with the networker's inadequacies and will frequently look for the first excuse they can find to end the dialogue. In such cases, they view networking as a nuisance and networking's reputation once again suffers an undeserved blow.

These abuses and misuses often lead to valid criticisms, and it is understandable that some might well be very vocal in their condemnation of specific networking techniques. These criticisms, *however*, are not an overall indictment of the networking process as a job-hunting tool. Instead, they are simply being leveled at the abuses and misuses of networking by those who are untrained in the fundamentals of effective networking.

There is a strong need, therefore, for job seekers to become extremely skilled in the process and techniques of networking if they are to become effective and successful in their job hunting efforts. The purpose of the following chapters is to help you, the prospective job seeker, develop the knowledge and skills necessary to become adept at this all-important job-hunting method.

Chapter 2

Why Networking Works

What is employment networking, and why does it work so well? These are two very important questions to answer before we delve into the basics of how to go about networking. If you're still feeling a bit hesitant about embarking on this creative and newfound method of finding employment, take a deep breath, and rest assured you're in for an important and eye-opening learning experience.

What is Employment Networking?

The general term "network" is normally defined as "a series of connected things." For example, a computer network is a series of computers that are hooked together in a system so that information can be shared between them. Through the network, then, the computer operator can access data from, or transmit data to, any or all of the other computers connected to the same network.

Likewise, a social network is a group of people that are somehow connected or affiliated. They are generally connected together for a common purpose or need. Most frequently, the reason for the connection is the need for either information or support. The objective of such social networks can be either personal or business related. Personal networks are normally comprised of friends and acquaintances, and are usually held together by common social and personal interests. Business networks, on the other hand, are normally joined together by the need to meet one or more business objectives.

Social networks, both the personal and business kind, are the very heart of the employment networking process. It is through these contacts (in other words, the members of the network) that the job seeker works to identify employment opportunities. It is the objective of employment networking, therefore, to access these contacts and to solicit their assistance in helping you find employment, for these contacts can provide you with job leads directly or indirectly (such as through others whom they know).

So, then, it is important for you to learn the proper networking process and techniques needed to most effectively use your personal and business contacts (otherwise known as your "social" network) to help you identify employment opportunities. Further, it is important to realize that employment networking is the sole method that can help you to penetrate the hidden job market and access those jobs that have not yet become known to the public.

An important point to remember is that networking is a powerful tool which, if properly used, has the potential to actually *create* jobs. The Granovetter study demonstrated that some 43.8 percent of all jobs found through the networking process were newly created and did not exist prior to the networking contact. Thus, employment networking deserves to be a major weapon in your job-search arsenal, and you need to become skilled in its use.

The Multiplier Effect

Part of what accounts for the power of employment networking is a phenomenon commonly known as the "multiplier effect." It works like this: if you had only the ability to contact those people you knew "directly" as part of your social network, employment networking would not prove very effective at all. It is the actual networking process, however, that allows you to expand this limited base of direct contacts significantly. By tapping into the social networks of others (those whom you know directly), in effect you access a large army of others who then become known to you through your friends. These associates are your "indirect" contacts, those whom you have gotten to know as a result of their connections with others.

If executed properly, networking can allow you to quickly explode a small handful of direct contacts into hundreds (if not thousands) of indirect contacts, all of whom become in some way involved in helping you with your job search. Multiplying these few initial direct contacts into a vast army of helpers can be an enormous force that can rapidly accelerate your job search and lead to a successful result much sooner than using other less productive employment sources.

Another way to visualize the networking multiplier effect is to think of cell division. Organisms grow by multiplying their cells. Each organism starts as a single cell which then divides in two. The resultant two cells then each again divide into another two cells (now a total of four cells). Each of these four cells then divides again into two more (now a total of eight cells). And so the process of growth continues as cells continue to divide and multiply themselves.

The networking concept is similar. As illustrated in Figure 2.1, you can start with as few as three direct contacts. From each of these three direct contacts (people you know personally), you then secure introductions to two additional contacts (now a total of six indirect contacts). Then networking through these six indirect contacts, you are again introduced to two additional contacts each, resulting in twelve new indirect contacts. As illustrated, by the time you reach the fourth level of contacts, you have enlisted an army of some forty-five persons in your job search.

Due to the multiplier effect, employment networking can allow you to recruit hundreds (and theoretically thousands) of people to aid you, in some way, in your job search. Effective networking is known to be an incredibly positive force and, as we have already seen, is by far the most potent weapon you have in your job-hunting arsenal.

However, the key to networking is an organized approach; if you don't go about it correctly, you surely won't get the results you're expecting. The mindset is simple: in order for you to realize the full benefit of this powerful resource, you will need to become knowledgeable and skilled in the techniques and subtleties of the networking process.

The "Obligation Phenomenon"

Although we have explained *how* employment networking works, we have yet to explain *why* it works. Although there are many nuances to successful networking, a fundamental element is known as the "obligation phenomenon." At the heart of networking is the referral process. Each time you talk to a new employment networking contact you eventually ask for a referral to others, who are part of the contact's social network. It is this very act of referral that is the glue that holds the networking process together and causes it to work.

When you tell another person that you have been referred to him (or her) by someone whom he (or she) knows, there is a natural sense of "obligation" to respond in a positive way. Although there is certainly no formal obligation to respond, the basic laws of society suggest such re-

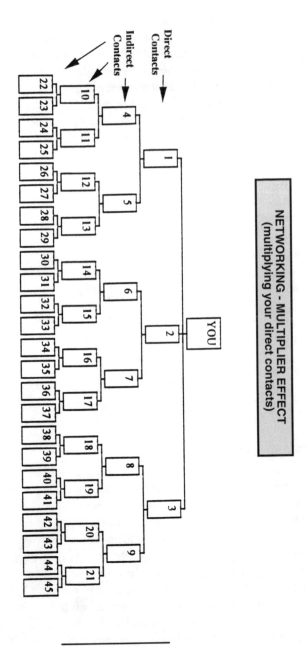

Figure 2.1

sponse is both appropriate and expected. To do otherwise would be impolite and could serve to offend or even alienate those in a personal network on whom we are dependent for information or some form of support. Being rude to friends of acquaintances is clearly not seen as acceptable social behavior!

Essentially, there are two different types of obligation at play in the employment networking process and on which this process heavily relies for its success. The first is social obligation, and the second is professional obligation. As you have likely guessed, a sense of social obligation occurs when you are referred to another person on the basis of a personal relationship that this person has with the person who referred you. A feeling of professional obligation develops, on the other hand, when you are referred to another on the basis of a business or professional relationship. In both cases, however, there is a clear sense of obligation to respond to you in a positive way. This is what is meant by the "obligation phenomenon."

To bring this closer to home, think for a moment how you would feel if you were contacted by a person who had been referred to you for advice and help by your best friend. Would you refuse? Of course not! Unless the request was unreasonable, you more than likely would go out of your way to be helpful.

Now think how you would react if someone contacted you for help as the result of a referral from a professional associate of yours. Again, would you refuse to help? Highly unlikely! Instead you would probably do whatever you could to be of assistance, within reason, of course.

See, referrals really do work, and they do create a very real sense of obligation to respond in a positive way. It is the referral process, then, along with the obligation to respond positively that is responsible for the success of the employment networking process. As long as your request for assistance is not unreasonable, you are likely to be greeted, in the great majority of cases, in a very friendly and professional way and the person whom you contacted will most likely do whatever he or she can to be of assistance.

The key to becoming an effective networker, then, is to make full use of the referral process and not be unreasonable in your request for assistance. If you follow these two simple principles there is a high likelihood that you will become very effective at employment networking.

Professional and Personal Influence

Everyone has a basic need or desire to be influential. People like to feel they can impact the way others think or feel about a certain thing and thus impact their viewpoint and/or their behavior.

Personal and business relationships are "transactional" relationships. This is to say that there is a constant exchange of information—a constant give-and-take of ideas, advice, and opinions. For the most part these transactions have a purpose, and that purpose is to influence others in some way. It is exactly this transactional exchange that encourages, builds, maintains, and strengthens relationships and the social networks they eventually form.

Networking is an essential part of building these relationships; indeed, in both personal and business relationships, networking is expected and desirable. In our daily lives, we frequently build and strengthen relationships with others by sharing information that is helpful to them. In turn, they reciprocate and the relationship grows and strengthens. Employment networking, if handled properly, is no different. It is a way by which we can request helpful information from our networks as a natural part of relationships with others on whom we depend and who, in turn, are equally dependent upon us.

The reality is that most people feel somewhat complimented when asked for their advice and ideas. They are pleased that you think highly enough of their opinion to seek their input, and will normally respond quite positively. It is all in how it is done and what you say to them. In final analysis, though, they generally feel good about the opportunity to positively influence your job-hunting efforts, and will normally do what they can to be of meaningful assistance.

The Mathematics of Good Networking

By now the mathematics of good networking should be quite clear: If properly performed, good networking is an "exponential" process. Each new contact is fresh and multiples itself. The net effect is that, in a short time, you will have a large number of people who are in some way trying to be of assistance in your job search. The larger this number becomes, the greater the probability that the right job is just around the corner.

Further, should you wish to stack the statistical probabilities in your favor, you will spend a high percentage of your job-search time actively engaged in employment networking. The fact that networking accounts for 68 percent of jobs found should suggest that this is where you need to spend your time if you are going to successfully conclude your job search within a reasonable time frame. Becoming skilled at this process will make it happen all the sooner!

Additionally, you cannot ignore the significance of Granovetter's findings. The power of networking should be evident when we stop to realize that some 43.8 percent of all jobs found through networking are "newly created" for those who bothered to make that networking call.

Finally, you can't overlook the mathematics of competition. Networking allows you to penetrate the hidden job market, the jobs that have not yet been communicated to the general public. This can place you in highly advantaged position since competition for these jobs is substantially reduced (or may be virtually nonexistent). On the other hand, if you focus your efforts solely on the public job market (newspaper ads, employment agencies, and the like), competition is significantly increased and the result is likely to be a substantially prolonged and frustrating job search.

The choice is yours. You can elect to ignore these statistics and suffer the consequences or conduct an intelligent job search that places the odds decidedly in your favor. The mathematics of employment networking simply can't be ignored!

Now that you know what networking is and why it works, you need to learn how the process works. The balance of this book explores the intricacies of this invaluable job-search method.

Chapter 3

Conquering the Fear and Anxiety of Networking

For those of us who work with people in career transition for a living, it is well known that the single biggest obstacle to employment networking is the awkwardness—the feelings of discomfort, embarrassment, and general anxiety that most people face when they contemplate networking for the first time. Clearly, it is not easy to pick up the telephone and ask someone for help in your job search. It is hard enough when the person on the other end is a close friend, let alone a complete stranger.

For the most part, job seekers are continuously haunted by these feelings throughout the job search as they pursue the networking process. Although the intensity of these feelings will usually abate with practice, they are always slightly below the surface and have a tendency to come forward whenever the job seeker feels the slight bit nervous or insecure. Nervousness and feelings of insecurity, however, are quite common for those going through the job-hunting process. In fact, you might consider yourself superhuman if you didn't occasionally stammer or find yourself at a loss for words!

It is important, that you acknowledge your feelings and deal with them in a positive way. This tendency toward embarrassment must be put to bed right at the beginning of your job search, before you begin the process of employment networking. Otherwise, I can almost guarantee that you will be subject to a form of "psychological paralysis" that will make it quite difficult (if not impossible) to pick up the phone and make those all-important networking calls.

It is the purpose of this chapter to help you understand and come to grips with the emotions that are, in most cases, sure to get in the way of your networking productivity. This process starts with realizing what these emotions are and what causes them. Having gained this understanding, it becomes far easier to control them and remove them as a barriers to your networking effort.

The "Beggar" Phenomenon

The majority of people feel quite awkward about the idea of calling others for assistance in their job search. Although frequently not at all reluctant to call these same people for general information or advice, there is something different about calling them for their help when you're unemployed and "down and out." For some reason this is seen as a form of "begging" and it can feel downright degrading.

A lot of how we perceive ourselves is connected with our jobs. For the most part we measure much of our own success by the position we have attained in life and our work-related accomplishments. Since we spend, on average, better than half of our waking hours in some sort of work-related activities, it is not unusual at all for many of us to see work as important to our identity and a key contributor to our personal self-esteem.

When we have been suddenly extricated from our familiar world of work, there is a sense of loss, and it is not uncommon to experience an "identity crisis." If such separation has been involuntary the feelings are even stronger. We have lost a certain touch stone, a key part of what has provided us with a sense of structure and order in our lives. In some cases, we have lost our sense of belonging and now feel an empty void in the place of what was once a sense of meaningful contribution and value. We have entered uncharted and troubled waters, and are now adrift in search of a safe harbor in which to put down our anchor and once again return to normality and a sense of well-being.

Now enter the world of networking!

It is not enough that we are already feeling a bit "off center," but now we are expected to pick up a telephone and call others for help? This adds additional anxiety to an already heavy emotional overload. How do we make these necessary calls, sounding self-assured and confident when we are still trying to deal with the gut issues that are continuing to eat away at our insides as the result of our employment separation? Certainly this is not easy, and these emotions need to be dealt with if you expect to be effective at the networking process. We will deal at length with these underlying emotions a bit later in this chapter, but first let's deal with this issue of the "beggar phenomenon."

As previously stated, our jobs are a key contributor to our sense of identity. Being meaningfully employed is a source feeling good about ourselves. It contributes heavily to our sense of value and self image—our feelings of self-esteem and pride. We are "proud" of our accomplishments and position, and they serve as a basis for our dignity and self-confidence as we deal with others.

Due to this relationship between our jobs and our self-image, most people feel that it is demeaning to be jobless and have to ask others for help. When employed, we feel a certain sense of independence and freedom. We are self-sufficient and need not rely greatly on others. It seems unnatural, then, to have to ask others for help. And, when unemployed, there is a tendency to feel that we are in a position of having to "beg" for their assistance. Pride can easily get in the way, and cause us to abandon networking for safer grounds where we can avoid the issue entirely and not have to deal with others. Thus, we begin to read newspapers, write letters to employers, send resumes to employment agencies, and use other far less productive employment sources in our effort to escape our fallen pride and heightened anxiety. This is definitely not the way to go! You need to confront these feelings and deal with them, if you are going to be successful in your job search.

Dealing with the beggar syndrome can be a relatively easy matter. It is all in how you approach the networking process. It is "what you do" and "how you do it" that can make all the difference in how you feel about networking. It can be either a positive or a negative experience, but you do have a choice!

The feeling of begging usually stems from the fact that people feel the purpose of networking is to "ask for a job" or a "job lead." This, however, should *not* be the purpose of your networking call. Approaching the call in this way does resemble begging, and it then becomes difficult to escape these much-dreaded feelings.

To avoid the feeling of begging, you need to reshift your priorities when you make these calls. Instead of asking for jobs or job leads, the purpose of your call should be to secure information and/or advice concerning your job search. In doing so, you are asking for "deliverables." Most people can and will provide helpful information and advice, and are only too glad to do so if asked the right way. Requesting such deliverables substantially increases your chances of a successful outcome to the conversation, and is commonly known in the outplacement/career transition world as the "indirect approach."

By contrast, if you use the "direct approach" and ask people directly for jobs and/or job leads, you place yourself in the position of begging for a job, and those feelings of pride and anxiety will rise to the forefront. Further, jobs and job leads are often not something that your networking contacts can deliver on an immediate basis. Therefore, they may feel awkward and embarrassed about not being able to respond positively, and simply want to get off the phone just as soon as possible. This is not exactly what you were hoping for!

So, the message is, to avoid the beggar phenomenon, use the indirect approach when making the networking call. Your contacts will feel far more comfortable being asked for things they can deliver—and so will you!

Embarrassment

Another emotional barrier that keeps people from networking is embarrassment. They feel embarrassed and ashamed that they are unemployed and don't quite know how to broach this subject with others. It is often far easier to simply avoid networking entirely and escape the situation completely. This is a big mistake, however, if you are hoping to be gainfully employed in the near future!

The source of this embarrassment has a lot to do with "how to explain the separation to others." This is especially true if the separation was an involuntary one. Whether fired for poor performance or simply caught up in a layoff or company restructuring, there is still a certain imagined social stigma that is frequently attached to being unemployed. In either case, we sometimes feel we have been singled out and, when caught in a major layoff, there is always a little part of us that feels that perhaps the company felt we were "not quite good enough" to retain. After all, isn't it true that companies always have a way of finding jobs for their good employees—those whose performance and abilities they value?

Yes, even the most self-confident and self-assured of us can begin to have doubts about ourselves at this point. I've seen it happen time and time again. I've seen highly talented, capable people, whom I greatly admire (and who are greatly admired by others) go into a psychological tailspin and take a nose-dive into a state of real depression. And often for no real reason at all! With some help and counseling along the way, however, they almost always go on to land a good opportunity with a new company, make meaningful contributions, and again ride the wave of success and self-confidence. Fortunately, for most this state of depression is both temporary and fleeting, and becomes (at some point) only a distant memory.

An informal study I conducted a few years ago seems to suggest that a high percentage of "involuntary employment separations" have little or nothing to do with the "ability to perform the job." Some 70 percent to 92 percent of such firings are believed to have nothing to do with the person's technical competence—in other words, the technical knowledge required to perform the job. Instead, most firings are "culturally based." The person's basic values, beliefs, and/or behaviors are simply not compatible with what the organization (usually the boss) prefers.

Since we are constantly dealing with people who have lost their jobs in our outplacement consulting practice, we are intimately familiar with this particular phenomenon. We have seen the same people (with the same values, beliefs, and behaviors), who were previously labeled "undesirable" by their past employer, move on to a new organization and become a "booming success." The only possible explanation can be that they have now found a culture that values their style, where their values and beliefs are in good alignment with those the organization cherishes and rewards.

My message here is that in a very high percentage of cases of involuntary separation there is simply nothing to be embarrassed about or ashamed of. This is a common event that has happened to thousands and thousands of others, and it frequently has little or nothing to do whatsoever with your value and capability. Chances are extremely high that, with a little help and guidance along the way, you too will move on to a successful career and far brighter days ahead. So, don't despair or be embarrassed by your circumstance. It is only temporary!

When you network, one good way to deal with the sense of awkwardness and embarrassment associated with your unemployment is "not to deal with it at all." Now, what do I mean by this? How do you network with others and not deal with the fact that you are unemployed. It's simple—just don't deal with it!

During a networking call there is no reason, unless asked, for you to reveal that you are unemployed. To avoid this, you simply advise the other party that you are "in the process of making a career transition" and are calling for his or her advice and ideas. In order to help you, the other person does not need to know that you are "unemployed" or that you have been "fired," so why reveal this information? To help you, all the person needs to know are your qualifications and the type of work you are seeking. Your contact doesn't need to know "why" you are looking. So, why tell them?!! If they feel they need to know, they will ask (and most won't even bother).

Good words to use when introducing the reason for your job search are, "I am in the process of a career transition" or "I am in the process of leaving Baxter Company." This leaves it wide open. Your contact doesn't know if you've resigned, if you've been fired, or even if you've left your employer at all. And, there is no reason for them to know this, is there?

Most assuredly, this avoidance technique will go a long way toward removing those feelings of embarrassment sometimes felt in the pit of your stomach when making networking calls.

Dealing with Nonproductive Feelings

In order to be effective at networking, you must first deal with the negative feelings that represent key barriers to picking up that telephone and making those necessary calls. If you don't come to grips with these right from the beginning, you will find networking most difficult and you will find ways not to do it. This would be a fatal mistake and represent a significant obstacle to the success of your job search. So, my best advice is, "Deal with it right from the beginning and get these negative feelings behind you."

We have already dealt with the issues of embarrassment from job loss and the feelings of degradation and awkwardness associated with the beggar phenomenon, but how about the issue of general anxiety associated with the employment networking process? How about those feelings of queasiness that you feel in the pit of the stomach when it's time to pick up the telephone and make those dreaded networking calls? What causes these feelings, and what can you do about it?

Having personally observed hundreds of people go through the initial trauma associated with networking, I am convinced that the key culprit here is the sense of the unknown. Most people just don't know what to expect when we make that call. So, they conjure up all kinds of imaginary demons to fill the gap. What if they don't like me? What if they won't help me? What if they hang up? What if they don't want to talk to me? What if they ask me why I left? They're busy and going to be annoyed with my call. And on, and on, and on, and on, only limited by the extent of the caller's imagination!

What we have here is a cut and dry case of fear of the unknown. When we are faced with a situation where we are uncertain about what will happen, our minds tend to go into overdrive and fill the void with all kinds of possibilities, only a tiny fraction of which actually resemble reality. Reality has, in fact, demonstrated the contrary—that most people, if approached properly and given the chance, are really quite willing to lend a hand. So, all of this anxiety is for nothing!

It is also a fact that when people feel they have control of a situation, anxiety tends to diminish considerably and often simply goes away. Due to their ability to control the situation, these people feel little or no threat, and are able to behave intelligently and rationally. They act appropriately because they feel there are no unknowns and, therefore, nothing to cause them to feel uneasy.

I find that the best cure for general networking anxiety is to eliminate as many of the unknowns as possible through meticulous preparation and training. If you are well trained and skilled at the employment networking process, you will feel less threatened and far more in control of your destiny. Good training includes anticipating most (if not all) of the barriers you may encounter along the way, and thoroughly preparing to deal with them effectively. Extensive training in such topics as "networking planning" and "countering networking objections" are covered later in the book precisely for this reason.

Simply put, careful study of the processes, strategies, and techniques offered in this book will put you in control of the networking process, and will consequently remove a lot of the unknowns and anxieties normally encountered by those having less-than-adequate training. I would wager that, by the time you are done reading, you will agree with this observation.

Explaining Separation Without Awkwardness

In certain cases it will be difficult for you to avoid offering at least some limited explanation for your employment separation. When networking with close friends, you will want to volunteer such an explanation and, in some cases, strangers through whom you are networking will inquire about the reason you left. In either event, you will want to be well prepared for this moment.

If you have been affected by downsizing, coupled with the elimination of your job, the matter is pretty straight forward. A brief explanation such as the following will suffice:

> *"Unfortunately, Doug, Baxter Corporation has downsized its corporate staff by nearly 20 percent, and my position was eliminated."*

or

> *"My position was eliminated as part of a 20 percent reduction in Baxter's corporate staff. Although offered another position, I felt it in my best interest to pursue other career opportunities outside the company."*

If you were offered another position as part of downsizing and job elimination, it is a good idea to mention this as part of your explanation for departure. This suggests that at least the company thought enough of your abilities to attempt to keep you by offering an alternative. This message is not normally lost by the receiver.

Now come the tougher issues. What if you were replaced by someone else during the downsizing or, worse yet, you were fired for poor performance? How are these issues handled when you are asked by your networking contact what happened?

If you were replaced by someone else during a company downsizing, things can get a little sticky. The obvious underlying question is, Why did they dump you, and not the other person? Even if this question is not asked openly, you can bet it is on the other person's mind. Don't automatically volunteer to answer this question, however, unless you are specifically asked to do so.

On the other hand, if you are asked why the company retained the other person instead of you, depending upon your specific circumstances, here are some possible answers you might want to consider:

> *"Jane had more time in the corporate accounting function and was therefore more familiar with the company's reporting requirements. However, I know this was a tough decision for the controller, since I had been a solid performer and a key contributor to the department's objectives."*

> *"My boss, John Weldon, told me he very much regretted having to let me go since, as my last four performance evaluations show, I had been a solid performer. Other than John's voicing*

his regrets, no further reason was given for the move. I know John will confirm my solid performance and will also serve as a very positive reference."

"Quite frankly, I was never offered a specific explanation for the move. However, I'm not really concerned about this since I had solid performance over the years and have good qualifications for making a contribution elsewhere. In fact, at this point I am looking forward to the change—which is really the reason for my call."

Note, in each case, how reference is made to being a "solid performer" or "strong contributor." This serves to shift focus away from why you were replaced and draw attention to the fact that you were seen as a valued resource. This technique will go far to offset the unasked questions concerning your performance. In this case, the best defense is a good offense. If your performance was reasonable, make that fact known!

Now comes the toughest question of all. How do you handle the question of your separation when you were fired for poor performance?

Obviously, never volunteer that you were fired. However, if you are asked point blank, so to speak, don't beat around the bush. Hit the issue head on! Here are some ideas:

"Sally, I'm not going to evade your question. Quite frankly, I was asked to leave. Since I have always had a good work history and have left an excellent performance track record with all of my past employers, I was stunned by the company's decision. Nonetheless, I find myself in the position of needing to move on with my career—which leads me to the reason for my calling."

"Very frankly, Keith, I was let go. There is no point in boring you with the details, except to say that I can provide excellent references from my co-workers, who are quite familiar with the quality of my work. Additionally, I know that my previous bosses at both Wilson Corporation and Du Pont will speak highly of the job I did for them. This current situation is unfortunate, but I need to move on with my career and find an appropriate job opportunity. I hope that you will be able to help me."

There is no easy way to handle conversations of this nature. If your networking contact insists on knowing the reasons for your departure, you are obliged to provide an answer. The above examples, however, will show that there are eight basic principles that need to be employed when structuring your response. These are:

1. Keep your answers short and sweet. Avoid the tendency to "over explain."
2. Never volunteer more than is absolutely necessary.
3. Be straight forward and positive in your response. Don't beat around the bush.
4. Be matter of fact. Avoid being apologetic in any way.
5. Always allude to other past work experiences which were positive and where you were perceived to be a valued contributor.
6. Refer to past performance evaluations that historically demonstrate your work ethic and solid contributions to the organization.
7. Where feasible, offer to produce references (other than your recent boss) who can speak to the quality of your work.
8. Be brief, and try to transition the conversation to the reason for your call—the need for help with your job search.

Although these types of conversations are never particularly pleasant, now you are prepared to deal with the issue of an abrupt departure in a positive manner. By employing these principles, you will at least be able to get through the issue relatively smoothly and be prepared to transition the call to where it needs to be directed—soliciting help from your networking contact.

Being well prepared to deal with this question *in advance* will do a lot to quell your anxiety. Additionally, you will find that after a few calls things will go increasingly smoother and most, if not all, of your anxiety will go away. However, unless you formulate an answer with which you are comfortable, you will find it awkward to talk to people and very difficult to pick up the phone.

Overcoming Fear and Anxiety

The best way to overcome fear and anxiety is to become fully trained and skilled in good networking techniques. In this way you eliminate a lot of the emotional barriers that get in the way of effective networking, and build a much higher level of confidence in your ability to be successful at it. To the degree that you are well prepared for networking, you will feel a great weight removed from your shoulders and you will find, in fact, that networking can be a very positive and rewarding experience.

Empathy and Self-Identification

Fortunately we are living in an age when being unemployed is a rather common event. With the rash of corporate downsizing (or "right sizing" as companies like to refer to their changes) in recent years, hundreds of thousands of highly skilled and qualified workers have found themselves in the unemployment line. Due to this wide spread phenomenon, there is hardly an employee, manager, or executive out there who doesn't have some degree of concern about his or her own personal job security and future. Today, there is a keen awareness of the ever-present possibility of layoffs. As these people have the opportunity to speak with job seekers who have networked to them for help, therefore, most will feel a sense of compassion and empathy. Often they are thinking, this could just as well be me!

The reality is, as you will discover from your own networking experiences, the majority of networking contacts will be quite sympathetic to your circumstance and will do what they can, within reason, to be of assistance.

Having personally worked with hundreds of persons in career transition over the years, I am only aware of a small handful of cases were the person contacted was rude or hung up. This is pretty amazing since I have been witness to thousands of networking calls!

So, my bottom line is, "Put your fears and concerns about networking aside. They are unfounded." Read the rest of this book, prepare, and then grab a phone and jump in! You'll find it's a lot easier than you might think.

Reciprocal Offerings

Before departing this topic, let me share one final piece of advice. Be alert to the opportunity to reciprocate for the help given to you by your networking contact. Always be thinking: "What do I have or know that might prove helpful to this person?". Whenever possible, willingly offer your ideas and assistance in exchange for the help that you have been given. This will be appreciated, will strengthen your relationship, and it will further reduce the sense of embarrassment you might otherwise feel when requesting their help with your job search.

We now need to transition your attention to networking planning, the subject of the next chapter.

Chapter 4

Planning the Networking Process

Over the years there have been many sayings that effectively portray the significance of planning as a critical factor in both organizational and individual success: Nothing succeeds like a good plan. At the core of every success is a well-documented plan. Planning is the bride of success and nonfocused activity the harbinger of disaster. These are but a few of the many mottoes that convey the important nature of the planning function.

Perhaps the best current example of the importance of good planning and its resultant success is the recent Gulf War victory over Iraq. Clearly the advanced planning of Generals Schwartzkoff and Powell (and their respective staffs) was the key to one of history's shortest, most decisive, and remarkable military successes. Can you imagine what the results would have been should these generals have sent their troops directly against the Iraqis with little or no advanced planning? You can bet there would have been a far different outcome to this military engagement without the several days of advanced air bombardment and the major flanking movement that cut off the enemy's supply line and retreat routes on the first day of battle.

As with any successful endeavor, the employment networking process must also begin with a well-conceived plan. Each individual networking contact needs to be viewed as a highly valued resource that cannot afford to be wasted. How effective this employment resource will prove to be in your job search efforts will depend on, to a large extent, how well you have planned its use. Advanced planning of the networking process will determine whether you either win or lose the battle for employment.

Ready, Fire, Aim—and Miss!

Too many times inexperienced job seekers jump headlong into the employment networking process without giving much forethought to the elements of effective networking and without a specific game plan designed to maximize the results of this all-important job-search technique. Consequently, they are not very good at networking and soon erroneously conclude that employment networking is, at best, a less-than-effective job-hunting source.

Normally, in these cases, it is not the employment networking process that is truly at fault. Closer examination will almost certainly reveal that it is a combination of poor networking skills and inadequate planning that are the root causes of such networking disasters.

To the contrary, well-trained job seekers who are skilled in the rudiments of effective networking and who have exercised a carefully planned approach are seldom heard condemning the networking process. Instead, their days are filled with fresh networking contacts, frequent informational meetings, and the kinds of positive activity that sooner or later leads to those all-important employment interviews. It is this group that is normally the first to identify potential employment opportunities and to land employment offers at an early date.

Where the networking process most often goes awry for most would-be networkers is at the very beginning. They frequently fail to put sufficient effort into the planning process to ensure the success of their networking strategy. Most frequently they are guilty of that old adage, "Ready, fire, aim—and miss!" The consequences of such poor planning are most likely to be heightened frustration, increased anxiety, and a substantially extended job-hunting campaign.

Nothing Succeeds Like a Good Plan

By contrast, those job seekers who recognize the importance of good planning to networking success are far ahead of the game. By carefully planning their approach to networking, they are clearly stacking the deck in their favor and substantially enhancing the probability of a shortened and more effective job search.

As an experienced outplacement consultant, my firsthand observations of people engaged in the job-hunting process strongly suggest that the results of effective planning can be dramatic. Through actual observation of hundreds of individual clients who have undergone career transition, I am convinced that those who have become particularly adept at networking planning are far more effective at job hunting than their job-seeking associates. On average, this "planful" group tends to find jobs much faster than others, and the jobs that they do find are normally better than those who are less purposeful in their approach to the employment networking process.

Planning the Networking Process

In order to ensure maximum effectiveness of the networking process, it is essential that job seekers thoroughly plan at two different levels:

- Macroplanning level
- Microplanning level

"Macroplanning" refers to the overall planning of the preliminary steps that lead to the point of making effective networking phone calls. Such planning includes the initial research phase used to identify specific industries, companies, and executives to be targeted by the job seeker during the networking process. The second component involves the identification and prioritization of the networker's primary social and business contacts that will be used to successfully gain access to these targeted executives.

"Microplanning," on the other hand, entails the detailed, advanced planning of each individual networking contact before it is made. It involves, among other things, an analysis of the networking contact's specific ability to contribute to your job search effort and serves as the basis for formulating specific networking call objectives as an integral part of your networking strategy.

Macro Level Planning

Taking a random or haphazard approach to employment networking can have serious consequences for the job hunter. Since, as we already know, networking accounts for 68 percent of job hunting success, it is critical to successful job search that people seeking employment be very methodical and purposeful in their approach to networking. For those who are truly serious about job hunting, the networking process is clearly something that cannot be left to chance.

Macrolevel planning is the first step in the networking planning process. It is macroplanning that serves to put in place the key building blocks essential to getting full mileage out of the employment networking process. There are six important steps to such planning:

1. Identification of target industries
2. Identification of target companies
3. Determination of target business function(s)
4. Identification of target functional executives
5. Identification of primary networking contacts
6. Prioritization of networking contacts

Without first defining the specific industries you wish to target for purposes of your job search, your networking plan will clearly lack the direction and focus required for success. Such lack of focus serves to relegate networking to a random, hit-or-miss proposition that will waste valuable time and resources. Conversely, a well-focused networking plan does not leave industry selection to chance, and thereby directs the efforts of the job seeker far more efficiently toward carefully thought-out industry goals that are both realistic and achievable from the employment perspective.

Once specific industry targets have been firmly put in place, it becomes far easier for you to conduct the necessary research to identify both the key companies and target executives who become the essential focal points of any well thought out networking strategy. Logic holds that, in final analysis, it will be these same target executives with whom you must eventually meet to explore employment opportunities.

Viewed in its simplest form, then, employment networking is the social process by which you make use of your primary contacts (and the social and business networks of these primary contacts) to gain access and eventual introduction to these target executives. If it is to be efficient, therefore, employment networking requires not only the research and identification of these target executives, but also the systematic identification and prioritization of your networking contacts.

Having researched and identified target companies and executives, the next step in the macroplanning process is to identify your networking contacts (in other words, people who either directly or indirectly can help you gain access to these target executives). Once identified, if networking efficiency is to be achieved, these networking contacts must further be prioritized on the basis of their potential for making such critical introductions. By prioritizing these contacts and approaching the most promising ones early in the game, there is an increased likelihood of early employment success and a much abbreviated job-hunting campaign.

So much for the "broad brush" on macroplanning. It is now time to get down to the specifics and look at a step-by-step, how-to process for putting this essential component of the employment networking process into place.

Identification of Target Industries

In the tight labor market of the 1990s, it is of critical importance for you to focus your initial job-hunting efforts on those industry segments where you are most likely to be competitive and realize the greatest probability for success. Naturally, in a buyer's market, employers are in the envious position of being able to "have their cake and eat it to." Not only can they find the functional expertise they need, but they also have the added luxury of being able to select qualified individuals who have direct, firsthand experience in their industry as well.

Although as a job seeker this is not what you may wish to hear, it is an accurate assessment of the state of today's job market. It is important at the onset of your job search that you temper your employment expectations with a good dose of market realism. In this way you will avoid establishing unrealistic expectations and remain focused on goals that are both realistic and achievable. Consider the following scenario:

If you were a controller of a company that manufactures automobile tires and needed a manager of cost accounting, wouldn't you have a strong preference for qualified candidates with tire industry experience? Why, of course you would!

Not only do such candidates possess good general cost accounting skills, but they also have specific industry knowledge that can contribute significantly to the effectiveness of the cost accounting function right from the onset. Such specific industry knowledge is likely to include raw material sources and costs, industry labor cost standards, the costs associated with specific tire manufacturing processes and equipment, tire distribution costs, the various tax nuances of tire manufacturing, and so on. With these added credentials, it would be difficult for an employer to give serious consideration to candidates from non-related industries who have lesser overall qualifications.

Why place yourself at a competitive disadvantage by pitting yourself against more qualified candidates who have specific industry experience? If you are to be effective at the job-search process and expect to successfully conclude efforts within a reasonable time frame, you should channel your employment efforts toward those industries where you have greatest value and where you can compete on an even playing field.

During the 1950s, 1960s and early 1970s, job seekers were faced with a much different labor market than today's, one in which the demand for talent far outstripped the supply. In such a "seller's market" it was far easier for job seekers to cross industry lines. Such labor markets were characterized by far less competition and it therefore mattered very little to employers whether or not a prospective candidates had specific industry experience.

Although not impossible to cross over into other industry segments in today's job market, most employment candidates will simply find it very difficult to do so. Whether or not such a transition is possible for you personally will depend solely on the demand for your functional specialty as well as and your ability to compete with others who have also targeted this industry segment for employment purposes. You need to be realistic in your assessment of both these factors before simply arbitrarily deciding to target industries in which you have little or no prior experience.

Begin by selecting and targeting those industries that are most likely to have an interest in your qualifications where you can be most competitive with others for employment.

Determining your ability to compete in a given industry segment is normally best accomplished by assessing your specific "value" to that industry. Your value is generally related to your specific knowledge and/or experience, which qualifies you to successfully solve certain key problems faced by most companies within that industry segment. To put it simply, it is your specific "problem-solving ability" that makes you attractive to such companies.

The self-analysis process, however, must first begin by examining the specific knowledge and/or experience you possess. Systematic review of your knowledge/experience profile will normally provide some good clues about those target industries most likely to have an interest in your employment candidacy.

I think you will find Figure 4.1 particularly helpful in assisting you with identifying target industries for employment networking purposes. This process, as presented here, should enable you to narrow down the field to those select industries where you have the greatest market value and where you will likely be most competitive for employment purposes. The process for accomplishing this self-analysis is fairly straightforward.

IDENTIFYING TARGET INDUSTRIES

KNOWLEDGE/EXPERIENCE CATEGORIES	YOUR SPECIFIC KNOWLEDGE/EXPERIENCE	TARGET INDUSTRY/INDUSTRIES
Raw Materials		
Products/Services		
Markets		
Customers/Contacts		
Processes		
Equipment		
Technology		
Laws/Principles		
Theories		
Methods/Procedures		
Other		

Figure 4.1

Note the column at the extreme left of the chart, headed "Knowledge/Experience Categories." The subcategories (raw materials, products/services, markets) listed in this column are intended, through the process of association, to help you identify "specific" knowledge and/or experience you possess that are most marketable to certain industry groups. By first listing your key knowledge and/or experience in each of these major categories, you automatically provide a good basis for defining your industry value. So, start the process by first listing this specific knowledge and experience in the space provided in column 2 of the chart.

Having completed column 2, then use the following set of questions to help you determine specific industries that are likely to have an interest in you as a result of your specific knowledge and/or experience profile. Record these industries in column 3.

- By virtue of your specific knowledge/experience in this category, which industries are most likely to have a general interest in your employment candidacy?

- What key problems will your knowledge and/or experience allow you to solve for them?

- In what way is your ability to solve these key problems unique or of particular value?

- How do your general qualifications compare to others with whom you must compete for employment in this industry segment?

- By virtue of your unique problem-solving abilities as well as overall qualifications, in which industry segments are you likely to be most competitive?

When performing this target industry analysis, don't neglect to consider secondary industries and/or organizations that are closely related to the primary industries in which you have worked. Such secondary targets would, of course, include industries that market either goods or services to the organizations for whom you have worked. For example, such secondary targets could include such categories as raw materials manufacturers, equipment manufacturers, distributors, consultants, contractors, subcontractors, and the like. Many times, your specific "insider" knowledge and experience could well be of interest to those companies comprising these various groupings.

Prioritizing Target Industries

Now that you have identified those target industries most likely to have an interest in your qualifications, it is important to prioritize them. Doing so will cause you to first focus your networking efforts on those industries most likely to employ you. The net effect of such prioritization will normally be a shorter and more efficient job search. For purposes of this prioritization, I suggest the following classifications.

Number 1 Priority
High industry interest—highly competitive with other candidates.

Number 2 Priority
Moderate industry interest—able to compete reasonably well with other candidates.

Number 3 Priority
Minimal industry interest—unlikely to be able to compete with other candidates.

When making a final selection of target industries for the purpose of your job search, I would suggest that you initially focus your efforts on those industries you have classified as Number 1 and Number 2 priorities. For the sake of efficiency, there is not much point in putting effort into those industries likely to have only minimal interest in your qualifications, and where you have determined that you are not likely to be able to compete successfully with more qualified candidates

Congratulations! You have now completed the first step in the macroplanning process. You have identified those target industries which will become the focal point of your employment networking efforts. The next planning step is to identify the specific companies that comprise the industries you have targeted.

Identification of Target Companies

Compared with first-time networkers, I must admit I have a distinct advantage when it comes to identifying target companies. As a consultant in the field of retained executive search for nearly 10 years, I had to made my living, in part, from my ability (or that of my research associate) to quickly identify a comprehensive listing of companies (and executives) within a given industry. So, I was forced to learn the basic research process used to identify target companies early on. This is not the case with most of you, who are learning this research methodology for the first time.

I was first introduced to this research process by a former colleague, Mary Murphy who, at the time, was research director for the Hay Group's international executive search practice (MSL International, Ltd.). As a research professional, Mary's credentials are impressive. An honors graduate of the University of Wisconsin with a masters in Library Science, Mary began her career with Dunn and Bradstreet in New York, where she advanced to the position of director of research. From there, she moved to a highly successful New York area executive search firm as director of research and then eventually joined MSL International (a major international executive search firm owned by the Hay Group and headquartered in Philadelphia), as corporate director of research.

Shortly following my employment as vice president and consultant with MSL International, I had occasion to request Mary's research services for the first time, in support of an executive search assignment on which I was working for one of my client companies. I still remember my absolute amazement when, only a day and one-half after briefing Mary on the requirements of this consulting assignment, she returned with an extremely comprehensive list of target companies and executives. I was very impressed with both the thoroughness of Mary's work as well as the speed with which it was done.

My curiosity raised greatly by this feat, I could not refrain from asking Mary how she was able to accomplish this in so short a period of time. She subsequently devoted several hours to training me in the use of her research approach, which I have used with great success ever since.

Obviously, the method that is used to successfully identify target companies and executives for executive search purposes can also be used with equal success to identify target companies and executives for employment networking purposes as well. Although the end use may be quite different, in both cases the research process used to identify these target companies and executives is identical.

The basic research process used in the identification of target companies and executives within a given industry segment makes use of two primary reference sources. These are *Encyclopedia of Associations* and *Directories in Print*. Both of these reference books are published by Gale Research, Inc. of Detroit, Michigan, and are updated annually. They can normally be found in the reference section of any good library.

The *Encyclopedia of Associations* is a three-volume reference source that lists some 23,000+ associations located in the United States. Among the various types of associations included are both trade and industry associations. Using the subject index provided in the encyclopedia, you can to look up those associations most closely related to the target industries that you have selected for employment networking purposes. Thus, for example, if you have targeted the pharmaceutical industry, you would begin by looking in the subject index for the heading "pharmaceutical" where you will find the names of numerous trade, industry, and professional associations having something to do with the pharmaceutical industry.

By reading carefully through the list of pharmaceutical associations, you will be able to identify those that sound most closely aligned with the specific industry segment you are targeting. You might find, for example, an association titled the American Pharmaceutical Manufacturers Association. Assuming you are attempting to identify specific companies that manufacture pharmaceuticals, this would appear to be an ideal choice.

In the subject index, adjacent to each association name, is a reference number. This reference number can then be used to go into the main body of the encyclopedia to find a fairly comprehensive description of the associations you wish to research further. Key components of these association descriptions normally include the following information:

- Association name, address, and telephone number
- Statement of the association's purpose
- Membership size and composition
- Names and titles of key officers
- Listing of key national/international meetings (sometimes including specific dates and locations)
- Listing of key publications available through the association (*including association membership directories!*)
- Price of membership directory

Since you will want to acquire a comprehensive listing of target companies from this particular industry (as well as target executives), your next step should be to phone the association's national office for more information concerning the contents of its membership directory. In order to properly assess the research value of this directory to your networking objectives, you should be prepared to ask the following questions:

- Is the membership directory available to the general public?
- Does it provide a fairly comprehensive listing of firms in the industry (including names, addresses, and phone numbers)?
- If not, are there other directories (not published by the association) that contain this information?

  (Note: Most associations will know this answer automatically and can quickly and willingly furnish you with the names and sources of such alternate reference publications.)
- Does the directory also provide the names, titles, and addresses of key functional officers of the member companies?
- If not, are there other directories (not published by the association) that contain such information?
- What is the cost and process for ordering these directories?

When you have determined that the subject directory contains the key information you require (primarily, a comprehensive listing of member companies, along with the names, titles, and addresses of the key functional executives you wish to target for networking purposes), you will want to immediately order the directory. To accomplish this, have a major credit card readily available (along with a Federal Express account number) that can be given to the order clerk. This will speed your directory's delivery, and you may be able to have it on your desk by no later than 11:00 a.m. the very next morning! Otherwise, it could take several days or weeks and substantially delay your job-search process.

In those cases where the directory is not available to the general public, or where cost of the directory is prohibitive (some cost $500 and more), you may want to obtain the names of nearby companies who are association members. Many times, by networking through employees of the local member company, you can gain access to the company's copy. In the case of larger companies, these directories often reside in the company's library, and are readily available just for the asking.

So now, with typically only a half-day of basic research using the *Encyclopedia of Associations* and a couple of phone calls, you will most likely be able to compile a fairly comprehensive list of the companies that comprise your target industry.

As an additional measure, however, I recommended you also use

Directories in Print as a cross-reference to the research performed when using the *Encyclopedia of Associations*. As the title suggests *Directories in Print* is a two-volume reference encyclopedia that lists some 14,000 industry and membership directories that are published by both associations and private publishing sources.

Since associations normally limit their publishing to "membership" rather than "broad industry" directories, *Directories in Print* often serves as a valuable reference resource in the identification of excellent industry directories published by outside (or non-association) publishing sources. Such directories are not likely to be listed in the *Encyclopedia of Associations* and may, in fact, prove to be substantially better than the membership directories available through the industry associations.

As with the *Encyclopedia of Associations*, *Directories in Print* also contains a subject index that makes your research rather easy. Again, by looking in this index under the name of your target industry (or industries), you will find a complete list of the directories available for this industry segment. There is also a reference number that can be used to locate a thorough description of the contents of these directories (as well as directory cost and instructions for ordering).

As you review the description of your target industry directories and/or call the publisher to get more information about their contents, keep in mind the same criteria that were used to evaluate the directories identified through the *Encyclopedia of Associations*. Specifically:

- Does the directory provide a comprehensive listing of the firms that comprise your target industry?
- Does it provide the names, titles, addresses, and phone numbers of the key functional executives you need to target for networking purposes?
- What is the cost and process for ordering the directory?

Again, by having a major credit card and Federal Express account number handy, you can likely order your copy of the directory right on the spot and have it on your desk by 11:00 a.m. the next business day.

By using a combination of both reference sources (the *Encyclopedia of Associations* and *Directories in Print)*, combined with some careful research and a couple of telephone calls, you will be able to quickly develop a very thorough and comprehensive list of target companies to use in your employment networking process.

Identification of Target Executives

Although the research process just described will normally suffice to provide you with a fairly complete listing of target companies, it may not necessarily provide the same degree of thoroughness to help you identify the exact executives you need to target. This is particularly true if you are new to your career and, therefore, need to target managers who are at a lower level in the organization.

Since most of the industrial directories list only the "top" functional executives of member firms, you may need some further research in order to identify specific lower-level managers to contact. Fortunately, this is not a particularly difficult task if you know how to go about it. Both the *Encyclopedia of Associations* and *Directories in Print* will prove to be valuable resources for this remaining piece of research.

Besides industry associations, both of these reference sources also contain comprehensive information about professional associations as well. As you might gather, in contrast with industry association directories (which are the primary sources for identifying key companies), the directories published by professional associations provide the names and titles of numerous (sometimes thousands) of individuals who are members of the target association.

Some carefully planned research using the membership directories of these professional societies normally allows you to easily penetrate your target companies and identify those lower-level managers whom you will need to target for purposes of your job search.

The specific process used to research and identify these lower-level "target executives" is practically identical to that used to identify "target companies." First, you need to determine the types of professional associations to which your target executives are most likely to belong. Thus, for example, if you are seeking a position as a senior sales representative, you should identify those associations to which sales managers and executives normally belong.

So, by using the subject index of the *Encyclopedia of Associations*, you begin by looking under the general headings of "sales management" and/or "sales executives" to find a comprehensive listing of professional associations concerned with sales. Then by reading the descriptions of each of these associations, provided in the body of the encyclopedia, you can select the specific associations and respective membership directories most germane to your specific job search and networking objectives.

For example, if your background is in pharmaceutical sales, you may discover that there are not only general sales management associations that are of interest to you, but also sales management associations that are specific to the pharmaceutical industry as well. The latter associations should be of particular interest to you, since their membership is comprised of sales managers and executives who are most likely to have strong interest in your employment credentials as a result of your specific industry experience. Directories containing the names, titles, addresses, phone numbers and company affiliations of such managers are obviously a virtual bonanza when it comes to networking contacts!

Again use *Directories in Print* to supplement the research already done with the *Encyclopedia of Associations*. The purpose of this additional research will, of course, be to identify privately published (non-association) directories that also contain the names, titles, and contact information of your target executive group. Some of these may be more comprehensive than the membership directories published by the professional association itself.

Unlike industry directories, which are normally readily available to the general public, you may find that a somewhat higher percentage of professional membership directories are simply not available to the public at large. Certain professional associations will restrict access to association members only, in which case you may need to get a little creative in order to access this information for your employment networking use.

Depending upon the specific criteria for membership, you might want to consider joining the association as a means of accessing these directories. In other cases, where either you do not meet the criteria for membership or where the cost of such membership is simply prohibitive, you should try another tactic.

In such cases, while talking with the association's national office, you may want to get the names and phone numbers of local chapter officers. Sometimes this can be done under the pretext of further considering association membership. Then a quick call to these chapter officers, if properly handled, can often provide you with temporary access to their copy of the membership directory. A friendly networking lunch can often turn the tide, and net you some additional valuable contacts to boot!

In any event, if you have carefully followed the research methodology outlined in this chapter, you are likely far ahead in the networking game. With a little planned research effort on your part and a few brief phone conversations, you will be able to prepare a comprehensive list of the target companies and executives who represent the leaders in your key industries. Your networking targets are now very well-defined and are clearly in your sights.

Your Networking Contacts—The Bridge

With your primary companies and target executives well defined, the next step in macroplanning is the identification and prioritization of your networking contacts. It is these contacts that will eventually lead you to your target executive group and provide you with the means for a personal introduction. These contacts are the social "bridge" that will allow such introductions to take place.

Now is the time to capitalize on the glue that holds the networking process together—the sense of personal or professional obligation created when you are referred to these target executives by someone whom they know. You will sense an unwritten social obligation and commitment to respond in a positive manner, and a favorable predisposition toward helping you in some way. This is a very powerful job-hunting phenomenon, and your personal contacts are the very vehicle through which effective networking will happen!

Preparing Your List of Contacts

As the next step in macrolevel planning, you need to prepare a comprehensive list of your networking contacts, the social bridges that will lead you to your group of targeted executives. In beginning the process of networking contact identification, you simply start by asking the basic question, Whom do I know? To facilitate this identification process, you may want to pull out your Christmas card list, your Rolodex, that pile of business cards you have been keeping at the back of your desk drawer, and any other organized (or disorganized) list of social, business, and community contacts you have. At first it may appear that you really know only a handful of people but, with a little help and prodding, the chances are high that you actually know a great deal more than you think.

Generally, you will find that your contacts fall into nine basic categories as follows:

- Close friends
- Relatives
- Neighbors
- Social acquaintances

- Social club contacts
- Church members
- Business contacts
- Educational contacts
- Community contacts

Figure 4.2 will help you systematically collect and classify your various networking contacts. By using this form as both a collection device and catalyst to spur your thinking along with the aforementioned lists, you will probably discover to your surprise that you actually do know a great number of people. It is not uncommon for some networkers to discover that they actually know several hundred.

This initial list of people (whom you know firsthand) is commonly known as your primary contact list. This list is your first line of defense and your starting point as you begin the employment networking process.

Take some time at this point, using Figure 4.2 to systematically prepare a comprehensive listing of these all-important primary networking contacts.

Prioritizing Primary Networking Contacts

Now that you have prepared this initial listing of your primary contacts, in the interest of networking efficiency it is a good idea to prioritize these contacts based upon their probable value. A column entitled "Networking Priority" has been provided on the form that you have just competed for this purpose.

When assigning a priority value to each of your primary networking contacts, you might want to use the following scale.

Priority Weighting Definition

Number 1
Target executives who can hire you

Number 2
People who know your target executives personally

Number 3
People who know your target executives professionally

Number 4
People employed by your target companies

IDENTIFICATION OF
PRIMARY NETWORKING CONTACTS

CATEGORY	CONTACT NAMES	NETWORKING PRIORITY
CLOSE FRIENDS		
RELATIVES		

Figure 4.2, page 1

IDENTIFICATION OF
PRIMARY NETWORKING CONTACTS

CATEGORY	CONTACT NAMES	NETWORKING PRIORITY
NEIGHBORS		
SOCIAL ACQUAINTANCES		

Figure 4.2, page 2

IDENTIFICATION OF PRIMARY NETWORKING CONTACTS

CATEGORY	CONTACT NAMES	NETWORKING PRIORITY
SOCIAL CLUBS (Members & Officers)		
CHURCH MEMBERS		

Figure 4.2, page 3

IDENTIFICATION OF
PRIMARY NETWORKING CONTACTS

CATEGORY	CONTACT NAMES	NETWORKING PRIORITY
BUSINESS CONTACTS		
Current colleagues		

Figure 4.2, page 4

IDENTIFICATION OF
PRIMARY NETWORKING CONTACTS

CATEGORY	CONTACT NAMES	NETWORKING PRIORITY
EDUCATIONAL CONTACTS Teachers		
COMMUNITY CONTACTS Politicians		

Figure 4.2, page 5

Number 5
People likely to have contacts in your target industry/industries

Number 6
People unlikely to have target industry contacts, but who appear
to have a large social or business network

Number 7
Persons unlikely to have target industry contacts, and who do
not appear to have many social or business contacts.

In Figure 4.2, a specific column has been provided for your use in assigning a priority weighting to each of the primary networking contacts that you have identified and listed. After completing prioritization of these primary contacts, using the above scale, it would be a good idea to reorder these (in accordance with the priority weighting that you have assigned), on the form for Figure 4.3.

By prioritizing these networking sources and listing your highest priority contacts first, you have taken an important step to adding a sense of order and efficiency to your job-hunting campaign. By starting with your highest priority contacts first, as you begin the networking process, chances are you will be far more efficient at making key contacts with your target executives much earlier in your job search. It will simply take far fewer phone calls to get there. This, normally has the effect of substantially reducing job-hunting time and allows you to identify and access employment opportunities far more quickly.

Microlevel Planning

You have now finished macroplanning and have put all the essential building blocks in place. You have zeroed in on target industry/industries, identified key target companies and executives, and have both identified and prioritized the primary networking contacts who will serve as the bridges in making these important contacts

The next stage in the networking planning process is to focus your planning at the micro (or individual) level. It is time to plan, in some depth, how to best utilize the contacts you prioritized, which is the principal objective of microplanning.

It is often at this microlevel that job seekers either win or lose the networking battle. By failing to properly plan their networking phone calls in advance of making them, would-be networkers often miss out on

---

PRIORITIZED LISTING OF PRIMARY NETWORKING CONTACTS

PRIORITY WEIGHTING	CONTACT NAMES	TELEPHONE NUMBER
PRIORITY #1 Target executives who can hire you		

Figure 4.3, page 1

PRIORITIZED LISTING OF
PRIMARY NETWORKING CONTACTS

PRIORITY WEIGHTING	CONTACT NAMES	TELEPHONE NUMBER
PRIORITY #2 Persons who know your target executives "personally"		

Figure 4.3, page 2

PRIORITIZED LISTING OF
PRIMARY NETWORKING CONTACTS

PRIORITY WEIGHTING	CONTACT NAMES	TELEPHONE NUMBER
PRIORITY #3 Persons who know your target executives "professionally"		

Figure 4.3, page 3

PRIORITIZED LISTING OF
PRIMARY NETWORKING CONTACTS

PRIORITY WEIGHTING	CONTACT NAMES	TELEPHONE NUMBER
PRIORITY #4 Persons employed with your target companies		

Figure 4.3, page 4

67

PRIORITIZED LISTING OF
PRIMARY NETWORKING CONTACTS

PRIORITY WEIGHTING	CONTACT NAMES	TELEPHONE NUMBER
PRIORITY #5 **Persons likely to have contacts in your target industry(ies)**		

Figure 4.3, page 5

PRIORITIZED LISTING OF
PRIMARY NETWORKING CONTACTS

PRIORITY WEIGHTING	CONTACT NAMES	TELEPHONE NUMBER
PRIORITY #6 Persons unlikely to have contacts in your target industry(ies), but who appear to have large social or business networks		

Figure 4.3, page 6

PRIORITIZED LISTING OF
PRIMARY NETWORKING CONTACTS

PRIORITY WEIGHTING	CONTACT NAMES	TELEPHONE NUMBER
PRIORITY #7 **Persons unlikely to have target industry contacts, and who do not appear to have many social or business contacts**		

Figure 4.3, page 7

the opportunity to fully capitalize on these valuable job-hunting contacts. All too often, job seekers simply pick up the telephone, giving little or no advance thought to what they are going to say. As a result valuable employment contacts are squandered, and the job seeker walks away having realized minimal (or no) benefit from having made the call. If you are going to be truly effective at employment networking, you can hardly afford to leave these valuable contacts to chance. Each and every person you contact has potentially unique and valuable contributions he or she can make to your employment effort.

In order to get the most mileage out of each networking call, you must carefully plan your approach such that the primarily focus of your networking conversation is on these key opportunity areas. Otherwise, you are likely to waste your conversation by focusing on nonproductive areas, where your contact has little or no ability to help. Worse yet, you are likely to ignore prime areas where this contact could have been of enormous assistance!

Analyzing How Contacts Can Help You

Before making your networking call, you need to "size up" your prospective contact. Give careful thought to what it is that this networking contact is most likely to be able to deliver (otherwise known as the "deliverables"). These deliverables, then, need to be the focal point of your conversation and the primary purpose of your networking call.

Actually, each networking contact usually has the ability to deliver assistance to your job search on several different fronts. Most first-time networkers don't realize just how extensive this help can be. The key to effective networking, however, is to focus only on those areas where the specific contact can provide the *most* meaningful help, and to avoid wasting valuable networking time by directing the conversation into those areas that will be least productive. Microlevel planning is the key to such focus and is therefore critical to the efficiency of the overall networking process.

Needless to say, you need to establish ahead of time in which areas each contact can be most helpful. To follow is a fairly comprehensive list of the "focus areas" in which prospective networking contacts can provide assistance. The following classifications should help you to decide what your phone call should focus on:

Job Information
- Specific job openings for which you qualify
- Specific job openings for which you might qualify
- Possible future job openings that may be appropriate
- Job content of potential target positions (where you are considering career change options)
- General qualifications for target positions (where you are considering career change options)

Target Industry Information
- Contacts with target executives who might hire you
- Contacts with employees of target companies
- Contacts with industry leaders (such as association officers)
- Contacts with those who serve the target industry
  - sales representatives
  - vendors
  - consultants
  - headhunters
  - accountants
  - attorneys
  - bankers
  - venture capitalists
  - financial analysts
  - accountants
  - attorneys
  - educators
- Knowledge of industry trends
  - general expansions and contractions
  - new products and markets
  - key problems
  - key opportunities
  - new legislation

- Knowledge of industry events
  - key personnel moves within industry
    retirements
    firings
    promotions
    deaths
    resignations
    disabilities
  - expanding companies (why and where)
  - contracting companies (why and where)
  - trade shows (national and regional)
  - association meetings (national and regional)
  - lobbying efforts

Job-Search Advice
- Resume format and content
- Job-search strategy
- Productive employment sources
- Interview strategy and techniques
- Creative approaches and strategies
- Career alternatives
- Industry alternatives

General Contacts
- General business contacts
- Community contacts
- Contacts with friends
- Contacts with relatives
- Contacts with neighbors
- Contacts with social acquaintances
- Social club contacts
- Church contacts
- Educational contacts

As you can see, there is a wide range of areas in which a networking contact can be potentially helpful. In fact, these areas fall into four main classifications: job information, target industry information, job search advice, and general contacts. Obviously, the first two categories (job information and target industry information) are the most valuable, and offer the greatest potential to assist you in achieving your employment goals faster than do the remaining two (job search advice and general contacts). None of these categories, however, should be ignored when doing microplanning. It only takes one good contact (regardless of the source) to land the right employment opportunity.

These general contacts (those not having connections with your target industries) are usually a lot less likely to get immediate results than are those networking contacts that are well connected with the very sources you are trying to reach. Job-search efficiency, therefore, dictates that your primary networking emphasis should be aimed at those networking contacts having target industry connections. It requires, on average, far fewer phone calls to gain access to your target executives using these sources than in networking through those who would appear to have no target industry connections whatsoever.

However, no networking contact (regardless of how apparently insignificant) should be overlooked in your job search. There can be some real surprises, where the person whom you least suspect to have a valuable contact just happens to know one of your target executives personally. There have been tales of barbers and beauticians making key introductions that have led to significant job offers, even at the senior executive job level. So, although you should certainly focus on the most likely sources first, never underestimate any one contact's potential to provide meaningful help to your job search.

Individual Contact Strategies

Effective networking requires that you plan *each and every one* of your networking calls prior to picking up the telephone. In this way you will be sure to focus your conversation on those areas where the networking contact is likely to be able to contribute most significantly to your job-hunting effort. If each call is properly planned, you should have identified both primary and secondary objectives in advance of beginning the networking process.

The following list of questions if used in conjunction with the above listed focus categories should help you establish the objectives of your call:

1. Based upon this person's occupation, position, location, or connections, what is he or she most likely to be able to do for you?
2. In what other areas might he or she be particularly helpful?
3. In what areas might this person be secondarily helpful?
4. In what areas is this person least likely to be able to help?

To facilitate effective microplanning, as well as to enable you to manage the unique record-keeping challenges of the networking process (which you will soon come to appreciate), you might want to use the networking call sheet (see Figure 4.4). These calls sheets not only help you better plan the objectives of each networking telephone call, but also provide you with a permanent record and ready-reference for all of your future networking activity.

I recommend that these call sheets be kept in a three-ring binder and filed alphabetically by the networking contact's last name. Alphabetical tab separators are another good organizational tool.

Before making any networking calls, it is important that you pull the names and telephone numbers of your intended networking contacts directly from the Prioritized Listing of Primary Networking Contacts (Figure 4.3) and complete a separate networking call sheet for each of your primary contacts. Start first with those contacts that you have classified as priority number 1 contacts, and then gradually work your way through priority number 2 contacts, priority number 3 contacts, and so on, until you have prepared a Networking Call Sheet for all people listed on this primary contact listing.

Besides the basic boiler plate information (name, networking source, phone numbers), necessary for each individual contact, it is vital to effective networking that you complete the two "objective setting" sections of this form as well:

1. Most able to help with (Primary Objectives)
2. May be able to help with (Secondary Objectives)

This information will become the principal focal point of your future networking calls and is absolutely vital to the effectiveness of your networking effort.

The networking call sheet provides a section that allows you to record networking activity and results as they occur. This section should be completed immediately upon conclusion of each networking call.

NETWORKING CALL SHEET

LAST NAME: _____ FIRST: _____ INITIAL: _____

NETWORKING SOURCE: _____ NETWORKING PRIORITY: _____

NICKNAME: _____ SPOUSE: _____

BUSINESS PHONE: _____ HOME PHONE: _____

BUSINESS FAX: _____ HOME FAX: _____

TITLE: _____ SECRETARY: _____

BUSINESS ADDRESS: HOME ADDRESS:

_____ _____

_____ _____

_____ _____

_____ _____

MOST ABLE TO HELP WITH: _____
(Primary Objectives) _____
  _____
  _____

MAY BE ABLE TO HELP WITH: _____
(Secondary Objectives) _____
  _____

DATE	ACTIVITY & RESULTS	FOLLOW UP REQUIRED

Figure 4.4, page 1

NETWORKING CALL SHEET
(page 2)

DATE	ACTIVITY & RESULTS	FOLLOW UP REQUIRED

Figure 4.4, page 2

This way you will automatically have a complete, up-to-date accounting of all conversations that have taken place with this contact source. Believe me, once you are in the process of dealing with several hundred people by phone, you will "thank your lucky stars" that you have taken the time to set up such an efficient record-keeping system!

Additionally, the call sheet provides a column entitled "Follow Up Required", that can be used to highlight any additional actions you need to take as a result of your networking conversations. By simply putting a check mark in this column, next to the specific networking activity to which it pertains, you have an automatic follow-up system that serves to remind you of any needed action you must take.

As each of these follow-up items is completed, simply draw a line through the check mark, signifying that you have taken care of it. Periodic review of the outstanding check marks (those that have not been crossed off), will serve as a continuous reminder of things that you still need to do. These can go on your daily to-do list , as appropriate.

If you have never undertaken a major telephone contact project of this type before, let me assure you that you will experience sheer chaos if you don't establish a good record-keeping system right from the start. After several hundred phone calls you will barely remember your own name let alone the three Jim Smiths who are returning your call. Additionally, you will have no organized way of remembering where key information (gathered from prior phone conversations) is located, and you will be continuously sifting through huge piles of paper for critical information that you need to have at your fingertips. So, a word from the wise—organize!

Finalizing the Networking Plan

You have now completed the overall networking planning process and are ready to begin making your employment networking calls. Although you can work directly from your networking call sheets when placing your phone calls, you may find it somewhat physically awkward to do so directly (due to the size of the sheets of paper).

Instead of calling directly from these call sheets, therefore, you may find it a lot more efficient to use four-by-six inch index cards, and the telephone tracking system described in the next chapter. However, the individual call sheets are an excellent permanent record of your networking activity and, if kept alphabetically in a three-ring binder, will be a welcome reference source as you need a more detailed accounting of past contacts.

At this point all the principal planning elements are in place, and you should be extremely well-organized to conduct a highly efficient networking campaign. All of the primary building blocks have been set neatly in place that will guarantee your ability to conduct an effective and hard-hitting networking effort. The only thing that is missing are the techniques for conducting an effective networking conversation, which is the subject of the next chapter.

Chapter 5

The Networking Phone Call

Although I have worked with hundreds of people going through the career transition process, including several highly articulate and supremely confident senior level executives, few are ever "entirely comfortable" with the idea of making networking telephone calls. Most approach their initial networking calls with a certain level of fear and trepidation. So, if you are feeling a bit uncomfortable at this juncture, let me assure you that you are not alone. For most job seekers, telephone employment networking is at best an unnatural act!

Chapter 3, Conquering the Fear and Anxiety of Networking, deals at length with the various emotional obstacles to employment networking. This chapter addresses the process and specific techniques that are so important to being effective at telephone networking. Hopefully, by providing you with some good techniques, some of those preliminary jitters will start to subside and you will begin to feel a little more comfortable with the idea of making your calls. But, if you're extremely apprehensive at this point, you may want to go back and reread parts of chapter 3.

Planning the Call in Advance

Without establishing basic objectives prior to making a networking call, you are comparable to an unguided missile—flying at great speed through the air but not striking anywhere near the target. The problem with this approach is that you can quickly end up spending all of your ammunition with little or no results to show for your efforts.

The same thing is true of telephone networking. Too often I have seen eager job seekers rip through their primary contact list at warp speed, only to have nothing to show for their efforts at the end of the line

RICHARD BEATTY'S JOB SEARCH NETWORKING

(except maybe a partially bruised ego and a bad case of depression). Few things can be more devastating to the morale of the job seeker and have such a negative drain on positive emotional energy than when "nothing happens" after working through the primary list of contacts. When this happens, though, it is a pretty good sign that little real forethought has been given to the networking process, and the networker has therefore failed to capitalize on the true potential of each networking contact.

So, in order to ensure effectiveness, you need to carefully plan each networking call before it is made. You need to clearly establish both primary and secondary objectives for the call, in advance, so your conversation will have clear focus and direction and you will get the most mileage from it. These objectives, as established in the preceding chapter, need to be pegged to those key areas in which the networking contact can likely provide the most meaningful assistance to your job-hunting campaign.

Telephone Record-Keeping System

Before initiating telephone calls, you should first establish a telephone record-keeping system that will serve you well in efficiently handling the high volume of calls you will be making while carrying out the networking process. Such a system is represented by Figure 5.1.

This system consists of a stack of four-by-six inch index cards along with three tabbed cardboard file separators, and a metal index file card container to house the whole tracking system. Most of these items are readily available for a few dollars at your local office supply store.

The individual index cards, as you can see from the example provided in Figure 5.1, provide space for filling in critical information important to making the networking call. This includes boiler plate information like name, address, title, company, phone numbers, and the like. Also included is certain other key information essential to making the networking call productive, such as the name and relationship of the person who has referred you to the networking contact. Also notice there is a place to record the networking priority weighting number, which allows you to prioritize your calls.

Importantly, in the center of each index card is a place to record both your primary and secondary objectives. These will serve as a quick reference when making each call, and enable you to quickly focus on those areas where the person you are calling can help you the most. In this way, despite the large volume of potential calls and call backs you

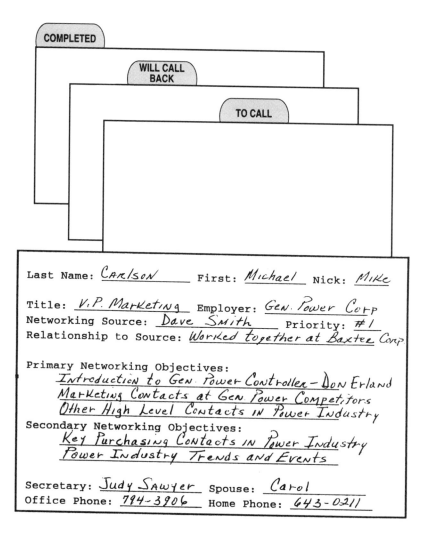

Figure 5.1

end up handling in a single day, the key information you require to maximize each call's effectiveness is at your fingertips.

In the previous chapter, you were provided with a fairly comprehensive process for systematically gathering the key information needed on these cards. You should use this information to prepare an index card for each of your primary networking contacts. You will also want to keep a supply of blank cards available for completion as each networking call is completed and new networking contacts are identified.

At the beginning of each day (and occasionally during the day depending upon the volume of new networking contacts developed), you should reshuffle the "to call" deck of cards so that the highest priority calls are always at the front of the deck. (The "to call" group, of course, consists of the cards representing individuals you are planning to call on that day.) This is easily done, since there is space for the priority rating of each contact right on the card itself. This way you will assure maximum efficiency of the telephone calling process since you will always be focusing your primary efforts on calling the highest priority contacts before those contacts having lower priority ratings. This serves to make you very efficient, and heightens the probability of employment success much earlier in the networking process.

Figure 5.1 shows that there is a tabbed index card file separator entitled "Will Call Back." This section of the filing system is for use in filing cards when you have placed several calls and have been forced to leave a message because of the continual inaccessibility of the person you are attempting to reach. In this case, simply file the potential contact's card alphabetically by last name in the "Will Call Back" section of your filing system for easy reference when this person returns your call. As a general rule, however, don't leave phone messages for target executives to return your calls if, with a little persistence, you could be successful in reaching them.

Finally, as calls are successfully completed, you want to retire the index card (alphabetically by last name) in your card file system in the "Completed" section. At this point, you should also complete a formal Networking Call Sheet (see last Figure 4.4), and record the results of your call for future reference. These call sheets then serve as a permanent, ongoing, detailed record of your dialogue with this networking source. These completed call sheets should be filed (alphabetically by last name) in an alphabetically tabbed three-ring binder for easy access and frequent reference, as needed.

You now have in place a great telephone call tracking system that will give you far greater control over what could otherwise become a totally chaotic process. By using this simple system, you will be able to control several hundred phone calls (all in various stages) at the same time, all with relative ease and efficiency. This will substantially improve your efficiency and overall confidence in your ability to manage the networking process. Believe me, you will find the results well worth the effort!

Critical Elements of the Networking Call

Before beginning to network, it is important to understand the critical elements of an effective networking phone call, and the specific role that each plays. Networking telephone calls, if done properly, follow a very logical and systematic process. This process is represented by Figure 5.2, and is worth some very serious study if you intend to become effective at networking.

The diagram in Figure 5.2 presents a kind of "systems approach" to networking. The networking call, as illustrated here, has nine critical elements which have been integrated into a certain logical, integrated process. Each element plays a critical role and leads smoothly and efficiently to the next. The end result is a highly effective process that, if used appropriately, will substantially improve your overall productivity as a networker.

To help you better understand this networking call diagram and how it works, I will systematically describe each of its components with examples so that you can understand both its purpose as well as its application. To follow is an actual networking phone call, illustrating the effective use of these critical elements.

The Greeting

The first step in the networking phone call is the greeting. Although pretty basic in content, the greeting needs to be positive, friendly and upbeat. The following are some examples of appropriate greeting statements.

Example A

"Good morning, John, this is Linda Swanson calling. How are you this morning?"

CRITICAL ELEMENTS OF NETWORKING PHONE CALL

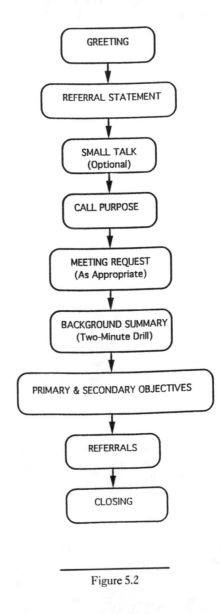

Figure 5.2

Example B

> *"Hello, Jane, this is Mike Loften calling. I'm calling you at the suggestion of- etc."*

Example C

> *"Hello, Mike, how are you this morning? This is Sandra Bevins calling."*

Referral Statement

The referral statement immediately follows the greeting, and is intended to establish the fact that you are being referred by someone whom your target networking contact knows. By establishing this personal connection at the beginning of the conversation, the contact is going to feel a certain obligation to listen more attentively and to respond in an appropriate manner. Here are some examples of referral statements:

Example A

> *"I am calling at the suggestion of Karen Freedman. Karen and I grew up together in Wilton, Connecticut."*

Example B

> *"Dave Stintson suggested I give you a call. I understand the two of you know one another from past Chemical Engineering Association conferences."*

Example C

> *"I am calling at the recommendation of Carla Johnson. She seemed to feel you might be a good person from whom to seek some ideas and advice."*

Example D

> *"I am calling at the suggestion of John Rittenhouse. John tells me that the two of you are on the Board of Directors of the National Manufacturers' Association together, and that you might be in a position to provide me with some good ideas and advice regarding a personal matter."*

How this referral statement is positioned, and what you elect to say, can have a definite impact on the degree of help your target contact is willing to provide. If the contact has reason to believe that you have a "close relationship" with the person who has referred you, there will probably be a much stronger sense of obligation to assist you. On the other hand, if the target individual feels that you barely know your referral, you'll encounter a reduced sense of obligation to help.

Consequently, you want to use the referral statement to not only state the name of your referral but, where appropriate, to briefly describe the nature of that relationship as well. Being able to state that you are close friends," "work together," "grew up together," or "were room-mates in college," for example, will usually be enough to establish, in the mind of the target contact, the relationship is a fairly close one, and he or she will be likely to respond with a greater sense of care and personal involvement than would otherwise be the case.

Where there is not a close relationship between you and your referral sources, however, you will not want to let on that this is the case. Doing so lessens the feeling of commitment to respond on the part of the networking contact, and your conversation will likely be far less produc-tive. In such cases, then, the trick is to infer (without actually stating) that you know the referring source well. This is accomplished by being clever in the words you choose during this stage of your introduction.

For example, by letting the target source know that you are aware of the specific nature of the relationship between him or her and your referring source (see examples B and D above), infers (but does not state) that you have a reasonably close relationship with your source. How else would you be aware of this relationship?

Another technique, as illustrated in examples C and D above, is what I call the "complementary referral" technique. This technique in-fers that you know the referral source rather well, since he or she has sug-gested that the target contact would be a "good person to talk with," "a good person from whom to seek ideas and advice," or "a person who is very knowledgeable about the chemical industry." This implies a rea-sonably close relationship with the source of the referral. Why else would this person be giving you such personal "good advice?" Addition-ally, since this technique casts the target contact in the role of an "ex-pert," it is also flattering and thus encourages the contact to respond as an expert by providing professional advice.

The beauty of these "inference techniques," is that the target contact has no way of really knowing just how close your relationship is with the referral source. Rather than to err on the side of being impolite, and risk rupturing an important social or professional relationship, most target contacts simply elect the "safe route" and assume that the relationship is a fairly close one. This usually results in a friendly and helpful conversation.

In some very rare cases (and believe me they are rare), the target contact may attempt to "qualify" the nature of your relationship with your source by asking how you know this individual. For example, your target contact might say "How do you know Sally?," "What is your relationship with Sally?" or "How well do you know Sally?" Don't allow yourself to feel trapped or exposed by the abruptness of such interrogations. Simply respond by saying, "We have a mutual friend, Richard Harper." (Harper is, of course, the person who referred you to Sally in the first place.) This response should be fairly persuasive of your relationship and cause the target contact to settle down into a more friendly and helpful mood. To push the matter further would be "high risk" on the part of the contact and border on "personal insult."

As you can see there are some real nuances to how you use the referral statement. How you position this connection with the networking contact will be extremely important to the success of your networking call. So, practice until you become very good at it, and carefully plan this statement in advance of your call so you don't "blow it" at the critical moment. Here, again, is where some good advance planning will have a major payoff!

Small Talk (Optional)

The next element of the networking call, small talk, is strictly optional. The rules for its use are:

- Use it if you are comfortable doing so, and it will enhance your rapport with the target contact.

- Avoid it when it seems unnatural or will do little to enhance your rapport with the target contact.

Small talk is informal, friendly discussion, positioned early in the networking conversation and designed to set a more informal, personal tone for the subsequent conversation to follow. If well done, and positioned properly, small talk will relax the target contact and put things on a friendly, informal level inducing the contact to "let his or her hair down" and share more of an insider perspective with you. The informal tone that it sets can be conducive to building a highly productive relationship where the contact will share such things as confidential information, personal insights about people or organizations, prized and coveted contacts, and offer to make personal calls and introductions on your behalf.

On the other hand, take warning! If you are insincere in your small talk or it is forced or unnatural, it could be deadly! Your comments may be perceived as insincere or shallow, suggesting that you are trying to con your contact into helping you. This insincerity can make your contact feel that you are somewhat superficial and not to be trusted, in which case it could become a major barrier to having a fruitful and productive discussion. Here are some examples of small talk:

Example A

"I understand from George that you are an avid skier. He told me about your recent trip to Vail, and your rather harrowing experience on the back bowls together. Sounds like you had a few heart-stopping moments near Sharon's Ravine!"

Example B

"Michele was telling me about how you and she used to work at Traxlers together between your Junior and Senior years in college. Traxlers was always a fun place, and I remember some great times I had there while working as a waitress during summer vacations in Ocean City. How did you ever come to work there?"

Example C

"I heard from Bob that you own an O'Day sailboat and spent your summers sailing the central Chesapeake. That's a great place. I have a boat at the Sailing Emporium in Rock Hall, and spent many summer weekends sailing in the vicinity of Annapolis and Baltimore's Inner Harbor. How do you like your O'Day?"

As you can see from these examples, it's pretty difficult to use the small talk technique unless you have some relatively intimate or specific knowledge about something the target contact has either done or enjoys doing. Also, it would be difficult to steer the conversation in this direction unless you are also knowledgeable about the topic and have something of relative substance to contribute to the conversation. Without these qualifying criteria, the conversation could seem rather shallow or pointless, and come to a sudden or awkward conclusion. In such cases small talk could result in a somewhat different tone then you had initially intended.

On the other hand, when used effectively, small talk can be a dynamite technique, and will normally set the stage for a highly productive conversation. By using it with skill and sensitivity, it can serve to rapidly transform what could otherwise have been a sterile, distant relationship into a sense of friendship and spontaneous warmth. The feelings of friendship engendered by such approach, if done well, will normally cause your networking contact to want to help you in whatever way he or she can.

To set the stage for small talk and provide you with the ammunition you need to make it work, you obviously need to know more about the target contact than just his or her name. When talking with your initial referral source, therefore, try to discover as much as you can about the person to whom you are being referred. You might find the following questions helpful in accomplishing this during initial conversations with your source:

- "Have you known Joe very long?"
- "How did you come to meet Joe?"
- "What is your relationship with Joe?"
- "What can you tell me about Joe?"
- "Do you know much about Joe personally?"
- "Do you know much about Joe's hobbies or activities, anything that would provide some personal insight about things he likes to do?"
- "Is there anything interesting you can share with me about Joe on the personal side—such as interesting things he has done or likes to do?"

Answers to these questions could provide some excellent fodder for formulating your small-talk strategy.

Once again, the need for some careful analysis and advance planning should be evident. Before routinely using small talk as a technique, be sure that you have thought it through—that you have done the preliminary research to set it up, that you know what it is that you are going to say, that you have some knowledge about the topic, and that you feel sincere and comfortable about doing it.

You will note, when doing advance planning, that both the "telephone call sheets" (see Chapter 4) and the "telephone call tracking system" index cards (described earlier in this chapter) have appropriate places for recording key information for planning small talk. Both forms allow you to describe the nature of the target contact's relationship with your referral source. You will want to make appropriate use of this during microplanning phase, as you also preplan the rest of your individual networking call strategy.

Call Purpose

The next key element is your statement of the reason for your call. This is best positioned right after your referral statement or immediately following small talk (when the small talk technique has been used). At this point in the conversation, it should be your intent to make it crystal clear to your target contact exactly why you are calling and to establish exactly what role you are asking this target contact to play.

It is frequently at this very point in most networking phone calls that, if not well-orchestrated, things can take a turn for the worse! Most of this has to do with the lack of experience of the average networker, and the common feelings of awkwardness and embarrassment associated with the "need to ask someone for a job or job leads." It is also at this point in the process that even the bravest of networkers tremble! Stay with me a little longer, however, and some of these feeling will likely go away.

When stating the purpose of your call, there are some excellent principles to follow:

- Never tell your contact that you are calling for a job or a job lead!
- Never automatically volunteer that you were fired or laid off.
- Never automatically volunteer that you have left your past employer.
- Always be direct and to the point.
- Always state that you are in the process of a career transition.

- Always use the name of your referral when introducing the purpose of your call.

- Always tell your contact that you are calling for his or her assistance.

- Always tell your contact that you are calling for his or her ideas, suggestions, information or advice, not jobs or job leads.

- Always be prepared to state that you are *not* expecting your contact to be aware of jobs or job leads—that is not why you are calling.

The following are some good examples of "call purpose" statements that can be used as the basis for modeling your own statement. As you read them, take note of how the above principles have been applied.

Example A

> *"Susan, the reason for my call is to request your assistance on a personal matter. I am in the process of a career transition, and Mary Johnson seems to feel that you would be an excellent person to speak with. She feels you would likely have some general ideas and/or advice that could prove helpful to me."*

Example B

> *"Mike, I am in the process of a career transition and, at Mary Gill's suggestion, I am calling to ask for some general information and advice. Mary seems to feel that, as a result of your position as a board member with the Marketing Association, you might have some interesting perspectives about things happening in the marketing field."*

Example C

> *"Glinda, I have decided to leave my position as accounting manager at Orf Corporation and am calling you for some general ideas in connection with my career transition. Doug Cooper feels you might be willing to share some general thoughts and ideas on this subject with me. I would really appreciate any advice and guidance that you might have."*

As you can see from the careful wording of these statements, there is no way that your target contact can tell whether or not you have left your current employer with certainty. The only thing that this person can know for sure is that you are in the process of a career transition. The reality is, it is simply not necessary for the contact to know whether or not you are still employed in order to help you. Why volunteer this information if it is not needed?

Additionally, by volunteering that you have departed from your past position, you begin to raise unnecessary doubts and questions in the mind of your contact. "Why did you leave? Did you quit in a huff? Where you fired? If not fired, were you caught in a layoff? If you were laid off, was it in part for performance reasons? Were you one of their less valued employees? These and other similar "red flags" are now circulating in your target contact's head, and you can bet that he or she is going to approach the rest of your conversation with an increased level of caution. The resulting conservatism could well get in the way of drawing out this person's best information and most valuable contacts. This could be a hefty price to pay for so small an indiscretion. Why stick your foot in your mouth, when all you have to say is that you are "in the process of a career transition"?

Much of the awkwardness and embarrassment connected with networking should dissipate once you realize that your primary goal is not to ask for jobs or job leads, but instead to ask for such things as information, ideas, and advice. If networking is done properly, job leads should be the *result* and not the *purpose* of your networking call. What will happen (as you will see later in this chapter) is, by using good networking techniques, target contacts will actually volunteer job leads and you will almost never have to ask for them. So, begin your conversation by making it clear to the contact that you are expecting his or her role to be that of an advisor.

As illustrated in these examples, it is good networking technique to repeat your referral's name as you state the reason for your networking call. This once again reinforces the personal connection you have with your referral source and heightens the contact's "sense of need" to respond to your request. Additionally, words such as "John seems to feel you would be a good person to talk with" are normally seen by the contact as complimentary and further encourage him or her to be responsive to your needs.

Meeting Request (Optional)

In those cases where you have reason to believe a target contact could be particularly helpful to you in your job search, and where it would not be cost-prohibitive for you to do so, it is an excellent idea to request a personal meeting. It is well known in professional outplacement consulting circles that face-to-face, personal meetings are usually far more productive than telephone call in achieving networking objectives. In these cases, you should plan to request such a meeting as part of your statement explaining the purpose for your call.

It is much easier to establish a personal relationship and rapport during a personal meeting than on the phone. Informal studies have shown that those who make use of personal meetings as part of their networking strategy tend to find an increased percentage of jobs through networking than through other employment sources. One major outplacement consulting firm, that strongly promotes such face-to-face meetings, for example, claims that 92 percent of their clients find jobs through networking. This compares to 68 percent for those firms who do not emphasize the need for such personal meetings. This differential suggests that personal, face-to-face meetings increase networking results (as measured by actual job offers and actual employment) by nearly one-quarter.

In deciding whether or not to request a personal meeting with your target contact, consider the practicality of doing so. In the interests of conducting an efficient job-hunting campaign, it is not recommended that you request personal meetings with all people whom you contact. This is likely to prove to be extremely time-consuming and not particularly productive. Instead, you need to be more discriminatory in your strategy, picking only those who you believe are best positioned to provide meaningful leads and contacts.

I believe it wise (from a time versus result perspective) to request face-to-face meetings with only those who are employed by or are likely to have contact with your target companies. Based upon the networking contact weighting system described in chapter 5, this means you should consider having personal meetings with those who fit the following classifications:

Priority Number 1
Target executives who can hire you

Priority Number 2
People who know your target executives personally

Priority Number 3
People who know your target executives professionally

Priority Number 4
People employed by your target companies

Priority Number 5
People likely to have contacts in your target industry/industries

The decision whether or not to request a meeting with your networking contact should have been consciously planned in advance as an automatic part of your call-planning process. Prior to making the call, therefore, you should determine the contact's priority ranking and then make a conscious decision regarding the potential benefits and cost/time practicality of such a meeting. Certainly those assigned priorities number 1 through number 3 should be given very heavy consideration.

In those cases where you elect to request a personal meeting with your contact, the request should automatically be positioned as part of your call purpose statement. The following examples demonstrate how such requests can be made:

Example A

"Nancy, I am calling you at the suggestion of Jim Duncan. I am in the process of a career transition, and Jim seems to feel you would be an excellent person to meet with. He feels you might have some general advice and ideas that could be helpful to me. I'm calling to see if we might be able be able to get together for a half-hour or so during the next couple of weeks. I would really appreciate your help."

Example B

"Bill, during conversation with Jane Reardon at the American Statistical Association meeting last week, she mentioned your national involvement with the Quality Association's Total Quality Committee and the fact that you know a number of people in the quality field. Since I am in the process of a career transition and have strong management experience in the quality area, Jane seemed to feel you would be an ideal person to meet with for purposes of getting an overview of what's happening in the field. I'm calling at Jane's suggestion to see if your schedule might permit us to meet sometime in the next week or so."

Example C

> *"Greg, Dave Johnson suggested I give you a call. I am leaving my position as Marketing Brand Manager at Walton Company and seeking opportunities in marketing management. Dave told me you have worked in consumer products marketing management for the last several years and would be an excellent person from whom to seek some ideas and advice. I would really like to meet with you, and was wondering if you might be able to fit me into your schedule sometime over the next couple of weeks."*

Hopefully, the above examples illustrate just how easy it is to request a meeting with one of your networking contacts. Here again, it is helpful to the positioning of your call to make liberal use of the name of your referral source. This serves to increase the target contact's feelings of obligation to respond appropriately. Also, phrases like "Steve seems to feel you would be an excellent person to talk with" are normally seen by the target contact as complimentary and certainly won't hurt your cause.

In requesting a personal meeting, be prepared for the fact that not everyone will be willing or able to grant one. In these cases your contact will normally cite a "busy schedule" and "workload" as the main reasons. Don't be personally offended by these rebuffs since in many cases the reasons stated may well be legitimate. Instead, be gracious and transition immediately into the rest of the networking process. Here are some examples of how this can be accomplished:

Example A

> *"John, I can appreciate that you have a very busy schedule. Perhaps, then, we might save your time by covering this by phone. Is this a good time to talk, or would you like me to call you back at a more convenient time?"*

Example B

> *"Since I am asking for a favor, here, I certainly don't want to inconvenience you in any way. Perhaps, then, it might be easier to cover this by phone. Is this a good time for you or is there another time that you would prefer me to call?"*

Example C

> *"Linda, I certainly don't want to impose on you in any way. Perhaps, then, it might be easier to discuss this matter by phone. Is this a good time for you, or is there another time that you would prefer?"*

If your target contact indicates this is a good time to have this conversation, then simply slip immediately into your background summary. You can do this by saying, "Perhaps a good place to start, Bill, is with a brief summary of my background." If it's not a convenient time, then you might want to use a similar transition at the time you call back and continue with your discussion.

Background Summary (The Two-Minute Drill)

Once you have established the reason for your call, it is most common for the target contact to inquire about your background and job-search objectives. Therefore, you need to be prepared to provide a quick synopsis of your qualifications and describe the type of position you are seeking. This is what is commonly referred to, in outplacement consulting circles, as the two-minute drill.

The two-minute drill is a brief description of your educational credentials and most relevant work experience, designed to give the target contact sufficient understanding of your qualifications, allowing him or her to make appropriate recommendations concerning employment possibilities. It also contains a brief description of the type of position you seek. It should provide just enough information to be informative, but not so much information that the contact will become bored with the description. Typically, this description should be no longer than two minutes in length—hence, the name "two-minute drill."

When preparing your two-minute drill, write and rewrite it until you have condensed it to the point that you can fit it on a four by 6 inch index card (both sides). This will force to you be particularly concise—to the point that you only include relevant, "need-to-know" information. Additionally, this has the added benefit of providing an excellent visual crutch for those first few networking calls, until you are fully comfortable with making this two-minute presentation. Here are some good examples of effective background summaries:

Example A

"Barbara, my background includes nearly 16 years in accounting management with major corporations in the chemical process industry. Following graduation from Cornell with a B.S. in Accounting, I went to work with General Chemicals in their Fine Chemicals Division where I advanced to the position of manager of cost accounting. In 1985 I resigned to accept the position of accounting manager for Davidson Chemical in Greenville, Texas. Davidson, as you may know, Barbara, is a $200 million manufacturer of agricultural chemicals and chemical intermediates. Some key contributions at Davidson's eventually led to my promotion to the position of corporate controller and, later, to chief financial officer of the company. In 1994 I was recruited by Dow Chemical to my current position as financial vice president for their Polymers Division, which is a $1.3 billion manufacturing operation. Barbara, I am currently looking for a position as chief financial officer of a major chemical company."

Example B

"Bill, I am a 1988 graduate of Penn State University, where I earned a bachelor's degree in Mechanical Engineering. Following graduation I went to work as a project engineer with James River Corporation in their Pennington, Alabama, plant in the Tissue Mill. For the next four years I handled major paper machine rebuild projects with a focus on the wet end of the machine. In 1992, I was promoted to senior project engineer and then moved to converting engineering manager for the mill site in 1993. Since then, Bill, I have managed a team of six engineers successfully carrying out over $50 million in converting equipment capital projects in the last two years. I am now looking for an engineering management position at the corporate level. I would consider appropriate positions with a paper manufacturer, equipment manufacturer, engineering consultant, or elsewhere, as long as the work is challenging and there are reasonable growth opportunities."

Example C

"Dave, I have been a senior accounts payable clerk with the Martin Company for the last three years. This requires my review, approval, and processing of over $3 million of vendor invoices weekly, without error. I have enjoyed an excellent reputation for work volume and accuracy, and have received high performance evaluations for all three of the years that I have been with Martin. Dave, prior to Martin, I worked in the Accounts Payable Department of the Baxter Company as an accounts payable clerk. I completed my associate's degree in Accounting at Borton Community College and am now looking for a position as accounts payable or accounting supervisor with either a manufacturing or service company."

As you can see from these examples, the background summary is brief, crisp, and to-the-point. It provides only the bare essentials required to communicate your general qualifications and job-search objectives. In most cases, this is more than enough to create a sufficient level of understanding for the target contact to respond intelligently to your stated job-search needs.

Primary and Secondary Objectives

The overall objective of the networking process is to get information, advice, and networking referrals. Contrary to the belief of most first-time networkers it is *not* to get a job or job leads. These are *not* the objectives of the networking process; instead, they are the "by-products" of effective networking.

New networkers almost always have a problem with this concept. Some, in fact, feel this statement is utterly ridiculous. They invariably ask, "What is the purpose of networking, then, if it's not to get a job?" Again, I repeat, "to get information, advice, and contacts." To this they respond, "That's only what you pretend to want, but what you really want is a job." "Not so," I reply, "I really do want advice, information, and contacts!" And so it goes—on and on—with many shaking their heads in disbelief.

Not to belabor the point, there is some method to my madness. What outplacement consultants have long ago learned is that you have to be more patient, subtle, and indirect if networking is going to work for you. Being asked for jobs and job leads is simply too direct for most target contacts. As soon as they hear these kind of requests, they tend to "head for the hills" leaving the networker behind scratching his or her head and wondering, What went wrong?. Let's take a moment to look a little closer at this scenario. There is an explanation for why the networking contact may act this way!

First, it is important to understand that requests for jobs and job leads are not things that most target contacts can readily fulfill, especially if asked right out of the blue. In fact, if asked too directly at the beginning of the networking call, the great majority of target contacts are unlikely to be able to respond with anything of substance at all. Consequently, they feel awkward and embarrassed and all they want to do is to get off the telephone! In essence, what you've done then, by being too direct, is shoot yourself right in the foot before you've even begun. And now, you've lost your valuable contacts who might have helped you, had you only given them half a chance.

What new networkers need to realize is that before they will be able to get substantive job leads, there has to be a kind of social-warm-up-period. You can't just pop these kinds of direct questions on a cold prospect, whom you barely know (if at all) and expect that he or she is going to produce! It's just not going to happen, and you are going to waste a lot of very valuable contacts along the way. There are, however, some solutions to this dilemma.

When approaching the target contact for the first time, be far more subtle and diplomatic. Be sure you have carefully navigated through the social-warm-up period before you begin popping your more demanding questions. Your contact simply needs to get to know you a bit before trusting you sufficiently to share key information and valuable contacts. Additionally, your contact will need some quality time to think before responding in a meaningful way to your deeper needs (jobs and job leads). So, give your target contact some breathing room, and don't create discomfort by rushing too quickly into the inner chamber for the crown jewels. Patience and diplomacy will get you there much faster than an outright bull rush.

The bottom line is you need to take an *indirect* rather than a direct approach when attempting to ferret out job leads. When using the indirect approach, you intentionally avoid asking for jobs or job leads and, instead, focus on such "deliverables" as information, advice and contacts. Unlike jobs or job leads, which are far more difficult for the average target contact to produce, the great majority of networking contacts can easily satisfy your indirect requests for information, advice and contacts.

By beginning the networking call by asking for these deliverables, then, there is a much higher probability for a successful networking outcome. First, it puts target contacts at ease (they do not feel compelled to get off the phone because they can't think of job leads). Second by requesting things that contacts can deliver, you automatically get them involved in the process of helping you.

As they begin to provide the information and advice you have requested, contacts begin to get more comfortable with the notion of helping you, and more comfortable with you as a person. As their comfort level increases, so does their trust. As the conversation proceeds and they get to know you better, they begin to feel much more "at home" with the idea of sharing key information and valuable contacts. Further, your patience has also bought the additional time often needed for your contact to remember specific things such as jobs or job leads.

There are essentially three major categories of information and advice from which to choose when establishing the primary and secondary objectives of your networking call. These are job information, target industry information, and job-search advice. When planning the objectives of a networking call, you need to consider what kinds of information and advice your networking contact is most likely able to provide. This, then, should serve as the basis for establishing both your primary and secondary networking call objectives.

So, before each call, review both sets of objectives as set forth on either the Networking Call Sheet or Telephone Tracking System Index Card for that particular target contact. This way you will be sure to focus your conversation on those deliverables that your contact is best positioned to provide. Areas cited as primary objectives should, of course, be the prime focal point of your conversation, with secondary objectives taking a second seat, and discussion ensuing on these topics only if there is sufficient time to permit this.

At this stage in the networking dialogue, these objectives need to be framed as requests for specific information and/or advice. Stick to requests for information and advice at the beginning—moving to requests for networking contacts only toward the end of the conversation (if these have not already been volunteered). Since there are a number of information and advice areas from which to choose, it is difficult to provide comprehensive examples of how to request these. Here are a few examples, however, from which you can probably model your own requests.

Example A

"Joan, as you view the food industry from your perspective, what are some of the trends you feel might impact my job search? I'm thinking here about such things as expansions and contractions, new products and markets, key problems, key opportunities. Basically, I'm interested in anything you feel might be helpful for me to know from a job-search perspective."

Example B

"Jim, as an industry association board member, you are probably in a position to be aware of some key personnel moves in the industry. Are you aware of an key movement in the senior manufacturing management area due to resignations, promotions, retirements, or the like? Is there anything in particular I should be aware of?"

Example C

"Debbie shared with me that you recently went through a career transition yourself. Since you were looking for a similar position to what I am seeking, I thought you might have some general advice about things that seemed to work well for you. Is there anything in particular you might recommend I try?"

Example D

"In talking with Barry, he told me that you had successfully made the career transition from chemical manufacturing to the environmental consulting industry. Since I am interested in making a similar move, how were you able to do this? Are there some insights that you could share with me?"

Example E

"Joan, as someone who has worked in the field of human resources most of her life, I'm sure you have some real insight about those aspects of the field that offer the greatest opportunity for professional growth. I would really appreciate your thoughts about what specialties within the field I should consider as a good starting point for my career. What observations could you share with me on this topic?"

Example F

> *"Carol tells me that you are heavily involved with employment of project engineering personnel for your company. I have just finished writing a rough draft resume for a project engineering position and could really benefit by having it reviewed by an experienced eye such as yours. Would you be willing to look it over and offer suggestions on how it might be improved? I would really appreciate your critique and ideas for improvement."*

Once you have moved beyond the initial stages of conversation during which you have sought the target contact's information and advice, you will then need to keep your job networking process alive by feeding it some new names and contacts. Without this constant renewal, you will eventually run out of contacts and the process will die. Since networking accounts for 68 percent of job search success, you simply cannot afford to allow this to happen. Securing these new names, then, becomes the next critical element of a successful networking strategy.

Referrals

At this juncture, you need to secure the names of additional networking contacts as well as the permission of your referral source to use his or her name when making calls to these new contacts. If you simply get information and advice from your networking contacts, and fail to also secure additional contacts and referrals, you have no basis for keeping the process going. It is paramount, therefore, that you become skilled at extracting new networking names from each source you contact.

In most cases, if the advice and information segment of the networking conversation is well carried out, most networking contacts will warm up to the point that they volunteer both contacts and job leads automatically and you won't have to ask for them. Although this is the ideal situation and does happen quite often, in some cases it's still going to become necessary for you to "pry" this information loose from the networking contact.

Here again, however, I would recommend against asking directly for job leads and would instead focus on getting the names of valuable contacts who might help you. Quite frankly, at this stage of the process, your contact (if willing to share such information at all) will normally have volunteered appropriate job leads. If not, it is highly unlikely that job lead information will be shared, even if you ask for it. So, why bother?

Instead, focus your attention on getting those additional contacts that you will be needing as the life blood of your ongoing networking effort.

There is really no subtle way to ask for contacts, so I'm afraid that this segment of your conversation needs to be fairly direct. It is for precisely this reason, however, that you need to position this inquiry *after* your requests for information and advice (the deliverables). By then you will have gone through the social-warm-up-period and your contact will be in the spirit to provide assistance to you. This greatly increases the probability that he or she will be willing to share the names of valuable contacts with you. The following are examples of different ways by which you can ask your contact person for the names of additional referrals:

Example A

"As I'm sure you are aware, in this tight market it's going to take a lot of work to surface the right opportunity. It is important, therefore, that I contact a lot of people along the way. John, are there people whom you feel I should be in contact with, who could be helpful in this process?"

Example B

"Jane, as you know, networking is the key to finding the right job in this kind of labor market. Are there people whom you know, through either your professional or social circles who, like you, know a lot of others and are well connected in the industry?"

Example C

"As you think about people you have met at past Manufacturers Association meetings, who seem to be well networked and know a lot of others? Are there specific people you feel it worth contacting?"

Example D

"Two of my target companies, in which I have a great deal of interest, are General Electric and Scott Paper Company. Do you know anyone who works at either of these companies whom I might contact?"

In asking for the names of key contacts, one technique that can have a great deal of payoff is the so-called "laundry list." This is a technique that helps your contact remember the names of key people (that he or she would not otherwise have thought of) through the process of association.

When using the laundry list technique, you should ask for the names of key contacts but, simultaneously, provide a "laundry list" of the categories or types of contacts that might prove helpful. Through association with these categories, your contact will often think of people whom they might not have identified otherwise. Additionally, while you are "rolling-out" the categories, so to speak, your contact has additional time to ponder your question and come up with additional names which, again, he or she would likely not have thought of, if under pressure to respond on a more immediate basis. Here are some examples of how this laundry list technique might be used to increase your networking effectiveness:

Example A

"Who are some of the people you can think of who know a lot of others in the industry? For example, Jim, people whom you know through trade association contacts, key vendors who call on you, consultants you have used, key professors, or others whom it might make sense for me to contact for networking purposes?"

Example B

"Barbara, as you think of people in the industry, with whom it might make sense to be in touch, are there particular individuals you could recommend? Such people, for example, might be employees of key companies, trade or professional association officers, salespeople, suppliers, consultants, educators—anyone you believe may know a number of others in the industry."

Example C

"Roger, as you think of various categories of people who might be helpful to me, are there particular categories that you feel could be helpful? For example, vendors, salespeople, consultants, professors,—people who know a number of others? Who are some of the people in these categories you feel it might be helpful for me to contact?"

As you can see from these laundry list examples, this technique has the potential to be extremely powerful in generating new contact names. My experience in coaching others to use it, in fact, has shown that it can become a very potent weapon in the networker's arsenal of networking techniques.

As new names begin to surface, think about how you are going to make these future networking calls even more productive. While the new name is on the table, so to speak, this is the perfect time to ask the referral source some basic questions that will help enormously to position that future call. Some of these key questions are:

- "How do you know Tom?"
- "Have you known Tom long?"
- "How did you come to meet Tom?"
- "What is your relationship with Tom? Do you know him well?"
- "What can you tell me about Tom that might be helpful to my discussion with him?"
- "What do you feel my approach with Tom should be? Are there specific areas where you feel he could be particularly helpful?"

As you can see from the nature of these sample questions, you have the opportunity to learn quite a bit from your referral sources about the person to whom they are referring you. All of this information could prove quite helpful to structuring the strategy for your next call. It provides ideal information to be used as part of your greeting or as the basis for some informal small talk. By using this information properly, it also strongly suggests to the new networking contact that you know the referral source quite well, heightening his or her sense of obligation to respond to you in a positive and appropriate manner.

Finally, you want to ask your referral source for permission to use his or her name when contacting the new individual. As you will recall, such "personal referral" is the glue that holds the networking process together and makes it work. In asking for this, you need to make it clear that you are not asking your sources to serve as a reference (unless, of course, they are familiar with your work, and this is appropriate). Instead, you are simply asking permission to use their names in the context of a "referral" only. This can be done as follows:

Example A

"Linda, would you mind if I told Bill that you suggested I call?"

Example B

"Although I'm certainly not asking you to serve as a reference, would you mind if I mentioned to Joan that you suggested I call?"

In the great majority of cases, your referral source is going to say yes to these questions. This will then become particularly helpful during that next conversation as you say something to the effect of, "Sarah Bauman suggested that I give you a call." Such statements, as we already know, provide that important "social linkage" so important to making the referral process work well.

In asking permission to use your contact's name, however, there is always the possibility that he or she might say no, that he or she prefers that you didn't." In this case you are on the "horns of a dilemma"— should you or shouldn't you? It strengthens your case to do so, but your referral source has asked you not to do this. What do you do?

Depending upon your personal feelings on the matter, there is a technicality here you may wish (or not wish) to take advantage of. Notice the way these referral questions were worded ("that you suggested I call"). Although it is "splitting hairs," rather than stating (during the subsequent call to the new contact) that it was "suggested that you call," you could instead say:

"Your name was given to me by Joan Smith. Joan seems to feel you would be a good person to talk with, since you have a lot of knowledge about the steel industry."

Although splitting hairs, you have not stated that Joan "suggested you call." Instead you are simply conveying that Joan had "brought up this person's name" as a "knowledgeable person in the field." You are not directly stating that Joan "suggested that you call" (although this is, admittedly, inferred). In any event, you will have to decide on how comfortable you feel with taking this tack, since for some people this might be seen as unethical. The decision is up to you.

Closing Statement

The final critical element in making successful networking phone calls is the closing statement. It is amazing to me how many people, after getting meaningful help and valuable contacts from a source, forget to express their appreciation for this assistance during the closing statement.

There are three main components to the closing statement. These are:

- The "thank you" statement
- The "resume transmission" offer
- The "future ideas" statement

Obviously, expressing one's appreciation for help is still socially very much in vogue. Thus, some ways to express your appreciation are as follows:

Example A

"Lee, I want to thank you for all your help. I especially appreciate your suggestion that I contact Nancy Greer and Steve Ellard. Both sound like good people for me to talk with. I really appreciate your help."

Example B

"I know what a busy schedule you must have, Chris, so I really appreciate the time you spent with me today. Thank you! If there is ever any way I can be of help to you, I hope you will give me a call. Thanks again, Chris!"

Example C

"Your advice and suggestions have been very helpful to me, Debbie, and I want you to know how much I appreciate your help. Thank you very much! I've enjoyed talking with you."

Although many consultants in the outplacement field recommend you tell sources you will follow up with them and let them know the outcome of their referrals, I am not sure this is such a good idea. Even though I certainly can't argue with the appropriateness of such follow up, I am concerned with the practicality of such well-intentioned statements. The daily world of the effective networker is literally filled with hundreds of telephone calls and contacts. Offering to get back to each and every one of them is simply not a practical consideration. Telling them that you will, and then failing to do so, is even worse! Now they think that you either lack basic social graces or that you are not very thorough with your follow up—neither of which impressions are particularly helpful to your image.

I recommend that you not make this follow-up offer lightly. Instead, use it with discretion, and offer it only in those cases where you are sure that you can meet your commitment. Also, reserve it for those individuals who have been unusually helpful, and where you have reason to believe that there is a high likelihood of payoff from their suggestions.

The same rationale pretty much applies to the notion of sending thank you letters. Although it would certainly be a nice gesture to send each of your contacts a thank you letter, you need to think hard about the practicality of doing so. A good networker will make in the range of 30 to 40 networking calls daily. Do you really have time to also get out 30 to 40 letters a day, without cutting back on your networking productivity? And, then there is the matter of the associated expense of paper, envelopes, typing, and postage. For a person whose severance pay may be running out, the financial implications of such a commitment could prove challenging at best.

This is certainly not to say that you shouldn't send thank you letters at all. Instead, I suggest you use some discretion and send them in those cases where they are really warranted. A heartfelt verbal thank-you during the networking call is certainly more than enough in the great majority of cases.

In those cases where a person has been particularly helpful, you will not only want to send him or her a thank you letter, but you will also want to forward a copy of your resume as an easy reference should they become aware of an opportunity for you. In such cases, during the networking closing statement, you should point this out and ask that your source contact you in the future should they have any additional thoughts or recommendations that would be helpful to your job search. Here are some examples of some ways this might be stated during the networking closing statement:

Example A

> *"Jean, if you don't mind, I would like to send you a copy of my resume for your future reference. Should you become aware of*

anything or think of any other ideas that might be helpful to my job search, I would very much appreciate hearing from you."

Example B

"John, I would like to send you a copy of my resume for your use. If you think of additional people with whom I should be talking, or come across any other information or ideas you feel would be helpful, I hope that you will give me a call."

Figure 5.3 represents a good model for use in crafting a combination "thank you" and "resume transmittal" letter. Notice how this letter reinforces the notion of making contact should your referral come up with additional ideas and/or contacts that might be helpful to you. Sometimes this letter's arrival can serve to jog a follow-up call with key contact information or ideas that your networking source thought of after the two of you had finished your initial discussion.

Sample Networking Call

The following networking call, although hypothetical, is very typical of what you might expect to experience during the real thing. Pay particular attention to how each of the critical networking call elements have been incorporated, and how the techniques discussed have been applied to increase overall networking effectiveness.

Networker *"Good morning Bob, this is Brenda Walker calling. How are you this morning?"*

Contact *"I'm fine, Brenda, how are you?"*

Networker *"Just great, thank you! Bob, I'm calling you at the suggestion of Bill Nelson. Bill and I are on the Board of EMA together and have been working on a joint project to improve vendor attendance at some of our trade show meetings."*

Contact *"I see. Have you known Bill very long?"*

Networker *"Well, as a matter of fact, I've known Bill for about eight years. We both worked together briefly at Union Carbide in the employment function."*

Contact *"I see. I haven't seen Bill for a few years, what is he doing these days?"*

SAMPLE "THANK YOU" LETTER

15 Fountain Lane
Bear, DE 18446

October 25, 1996

Mr. Joseph P. Danner
Brand Manager
Braxton Foods, Inc.
300 East Main Street
Wilmington, DE 18355

Dear Joe:

Thank you very much for your help with my job search today. It was nice of you to take the time to be of assistance, and I really appreciated your thoughtfulness. Hopefully, at some point in the future, I may have the opportunity to return the favor.

Joe, I especially appreciated your sharing with me the names of Sally Johnson and Duke Carlson. Both seem to be well connected in the industry, and I look forward to my conversations with them. Additionally, your overview of some of the current trends in the food industry was particularly enlightening.

By way of staying in touch, I have enclosed a copy of my resume for your reference. Should you have any additional ideas concerning my job search, or think of others with whom I should be in contact, I would very much appreciate hearing from you.

Thanks again, Joe, for your kindness.

Sincerely,

Linda Ballard

Linda P. Ballard

Figure 5.3

Networker *"He's working for the Braxton Company as director of employment and seems to like it very much."*

Contact *"That's great. I've always liked Bill, and I'm glad he is doing well. Brenda, what can I do for you?"*

Networker *"Bob, I'm in the process of a career transition and I've targeted several companies in the food industry for my job search. Bill says you've been working in the industry for several years and may have some ideas for me."*

Contact *"I see. Why don't you tell me a little about yourself."*

Networker *"Sure, I'd be happy to."*

[pause]

"Bob, I'm a graduate of Boston College with a bachelor's degree in Business Psychology. During the earlier part of my career I was with Union Carbide in a wide range of positions in Human Resources. This included an early assignment as a management intern at one of their chemical manufacturing facilities in East Windsor, Connecticut, followed by a series of generalist assignments at the plant level. In 1988 I moved to corporate headquarters, where I was promoted to manager of technical employment for the corporation. In fact, this was when I met Bill. Over the next five years, I rotated through the administrative, marketing and sales employment areas and was eventually promoted to director of corporate employment in 1992. Finally, last year I was recruited away by General Instrument Corporation as vice president of human resources for one of their business units.

"At this point, however, I want to return to the employment world at a senior level for either a large corporation or a major search firm. I am particularly attracted to the food industry and know from Bill you might have some insight about things going on in the industry that could impact my job search. I was wondering whether your schedule might allow us to get together sometime over the next couple of weeks."

Contact *"Gee, I'd like to accommodate you, Brenda, but my schedule is impossible for the next several weeks and I'd really be hard-pressed to set up a meeting."*

Networker   *"No problem, Bob, I certainly don't want to inconvenience you. Perhaps we can cover this on the phone. Is this a good time for you, or would you rather have me call you back?"*

Contact   *"Actually, this is probably as good a time as ever. Is there anything in particular that you would like to know about the food industry?"*

Networker   *"Yes, I'm interested in several things. Specifically, I'd like to know something about the current state of the industry—things like the general condition of the industry, major expansion and contractions, firms that seem like they are on the move, key problems and opportunities, and anything else you feel it might be helpful for me to know from a job-search standpoint. Perhaps a good place to start would be with general industry conditions."*

Contact   *"Well, Brenda, I'm not exactly sure whether this is going to be what want you want to hear, but the industry has been hit hard by the current recession, and a number of the key firms have been cutting back. There doesn't appear to be a lot of hiring going on in the industry."*

Networker   *"You're right, I was hoping to hear a more optimistic report. But, I guess I'm really not that surprised, since most consumer products companies appear to have been hit fairly hard by the recession. Are there any companies that seem to be the exception to the rule?"*

Contact   *"Yes, American Foods Corporation continues to do well. They have gobbled up Dexter Foods, Blair Pickle Corporation, and three meat processors in the last year alone. They appear to be on their way to becoming a dominant force in the industry within the next year or two."*

Networker   *"Wow, that's interesting! Do you know anyone that works at American, I might contact?"*

Contact   *" Yes, I know two people quite well—Walt Kimbler and Steve Bassett. Both are in the marketing group."*

Networker   *"Do you think it might be worthwhile to give them a call?"*

Contact   *"It's hard to tell, but it might be worth a try."*

Networker   *"How did you come to know Walt and Steve?"*

Contact   *"Actually, it's a long story, but our families vacationed near one another at Duck on the Outter Banks and one day on the beach we struck up a conversation that led to an invitation to play cards at Walt's place. We've been playing cards every summer ever since."*

Networker   *"That's an interesting story. When I call Walt and Steve, would you mind if I told them that you suggested I call?"*

Contact   *"No, not at all. In fact, tell them I'm looking forward to our next round of poker this summer."*

Networker   *"Sure will!"*

[pause]

"Bob, are there other people who are well networked in the food industry, who you feel it would be helpful for me to get to know? For example, how about other marketing executives you've gotten to know through your professional or trade associations?"

Contact   *"Yes, you should call Peggy Jordan. She's membership director for the Food Marketing Association and knows everybody worth knowing in the industry. She would also have a pretty good idea about what's happening in the industry as well. Peggy's a key player who moves in all the right circles. She's also a good buddy as well, so tell her I said hello. Let me get her phone number for you."*

Networker   *"Thanks, I appreciate that! Bob, how about others you know in the industry. For example, how about consultants, equipment vendors, distributors, or others who seem well connected?"*

Contact   *"You may want to give George Mason a call at Processing Equipment Corporation. His number is (205) 779-2493. George is general manager of the southern region and knows a lot of people in the food industry along the eastern seaboard. He sells equipment to most of them. He would be a good guy to talk with."*

Networker   *"Great, sounds like a winner! Is it okay to use your name?"*

Contact   *"Sure, no problem. I think he will remember me."*

[pause]

"Listen, I hate to do this, but I'm due at a staff meeting in about five minutes, and need to run."

Networker   *"No problem, Bob. Don't let me hold you up." "Listen though, I really appreciate your help. Thanks for the names and your observations about the industry. This has been very helpful, and I really appreciate it."*

[pause]

"Also, if you don't mind, I'll send you a copy of my resume. That way if you have any additional ideas or think of anyone else I should be talking with, you'll be able to give me a call."

Contact   *"I'd be happy to!"*

Networker   *"Thanks again, Bob."*

Contact   *"My pleasure, Brenda."*

Networker   *"Good-bye."*

Contact   *"Good-bye."*

Chapter 6

The Networking Meeting

Statistics suggest that personal meetings with networking contacts are likely to be more productive than networking by telephone. In fact, data from one nationally known outplacement consulting firm, Challenger, Gray & Christmas, suggests that there can be a 25 percent increased improvement in networking results as the result of such face-to-face meetings.

Although this statistic is impressive and should give job seekers good cause to set up such face-to-face meetings with networking contacts, I recommend in the interest of job-search efficiency that some discretion be exercised in choosing those specific networking sources with whom you elect to meet. Not all such meetings will prove productive.

When engaged in a job search, you are always working against the clock. Time is of the essence. What you elect to do, and when you elect to do it, can have significant impact on the length of time it will take you to successfully complete your job-search mission. This is particularly true of networking meetings, which can individually consume considerable chunks of valuable job-hunting time, if not properly planned or if such meetings are arranged with persons who can contribute little to your overall effort.

Someone who is working diligently at networking can easily make between 30 to 40 telephone calls daily. By contrast, a good networker can normally conduct, at best, only two to three effective networking meetings within the same time frame. As a result, considerable time can be lost when these meetings have been set up with the wrong people or the networker fails to capitalize on the meeting due to inadequate planning.

Planning the Meeting

The first consideration when planning a networking meeting, is to decide whether or not the meeting should even occur in the first place. Obviously, meeting with individuals who can do little or nothing to assist you in your job search is not constructive use of your time. Such meetings, although they may be socially satisfying and consoling, will divert your efforts from other networking sources having far greater potential to provide meaningful job-hunting assistance.

Generally, face-to-face networking meetings should only be arranged with those contacts who have reasonable probability of providing meaningful assistance. I suggest you reserve such personal meetings for those individuals who fit one or more of the following classifications:

- Target executives who can hire you
- People who know your target executives personally
- People who know your target executives professionally
- People employed by your target company
- Persons with contacts in your target industry

Sound familiar? It should, since these are the first five classifications (introduced in chapter 4) used to prioritize networking contacts based on their relative job-search value.

Clearly there is little gained from taking time to meet with people who have no connection whatsoever with either your target industry or target companies. Decisions to hold networking meeting with such persons ,as a routine practice, is bound to have dire consequences on job search efficiency and the length of time to successfully conclude the job-hunt. So, the rule of thumb, when deciding with whom you should meet, is to stick with only those individuals who have connections with your target industries. This will at least ensure that you will come away from your meeting with fresh new target industry contacts to add to your networking list. Anything short of this is probably simply not worth the effort and will only prolong your job-hunting campaign.

Of course, the two exceptions to this rule are "informational meetings" intended to provide you with specific advice in two key areas:

1. Resume preparation and job-hunting strategy
2. Career change advice

Be sure, if you elect to meet with professionals to secure information in these two important areas, however, that they are truly an "expert" on the topic, and that you will not be misled by a well-meaning novice. Carefully research the credentials of these contacts in advance, so that your time will be well-spent and ensure that you will be getting valid advice from someone who truly knows.

Informational meetings to secure job-hunting and/or career change advice are normally conducted during the initial research phase of your job search. Once these facets of your overall job-hunting strategy are in place, however, there should normally be no need to conduct further networking meetings of this type. The focus of your networking meetings are intended to provide you with valuable target industry contacts and eventual job leads.

If networking meetings are to have maximum payoff, they must not only be with the right persons, but they must also be well planned. You must have specific meeting objectives and an appropriate agenda planned in order to fully capitalize on the time you invest with your networking contact. In this way, conversation should be highly focused on those topics most likely to provide greatest benefit to your overall job-hunting effort. By contrast, without such planning and focus, networking conversations are likely to stray into areas where your contacts are least qualified to provide you with meaningful help, and your time will be wasted.

Planning Meeting Agenda

Effective face-to-face networking meetings start with having a good meeting agenda planned in advance of your meeting with the networking contact. Both the specific objectives as well as the content of this agenda will, of course, vary with the nature of the meeting and the type of networking contact. However, both need to be carefully thought-out in advance in order to ensure an efficient and productive discussion.

Figure 6.1 provides a good planning tool to assist you properly with orchestrating a productive meeting with a networking contact. This form helps you logically think through the nature of the contact person's position and contacts, and assists you in formulating a meeting agenda that is most likely to prove beneficial to you and your overall job-search objectives.

NETWORKING MEETING PLAN

NAME: _____   MEETING DATE: _____
JOB TITLE: _____   MEETING TIME: _____
EMPLOYER: _____

REFERRAL SOURCE: _____
RELATIONSHIP WITH SOURCE: _____
_____

AREAS WHERE CONTACT CAN MOST CONTRIBUTE:
(Check Those That Apply)

- [ ] Target Executive Who Can Hire Me
- [ ] Introductions to Target Executives
- [ ] Introductions to Target Company Employees
- [ ] Key Personnel Moves in Target Industry
- [ ] General Knowledge - Target Industry Trends & Events
- [ ] Job Search Advice
- [ ] Career Advice

MEETING AGENDA:

Primary Agenda:

1. _____
2. _____
3. _____
4. _____

Secondary Agenda:

1. _____
2. _____

Figure 6.1

As suggested by this planning form, key networking contacts can play one (or more) of seven possible roles in helping you with your job search. These people:

1. Can hire you
2. Can provide introductions to target executives
3. Can provide introductions to target company employees
4. Can advise you of key personnel moves in target industry
5. Can provide general information on target industry trends and events
6. Can provide job-search advice
7. Can provide career advice

Using the planning form, first check those areas where a particular contact is most likely to be able to help you. Then, based upon this person's position and knowledge of the industry, select as your primary agenda those areas where you believe this contact can provide you with the greatest assistance. List these areas, in order of priority, under the heading Primary Agenda. Then, identify those secondary areas where you believe that the networking contact is likely to be able to provide modest assistance, and list them on the planning form under the heading "Secondary Agenda." You now have in place a very focused meeting agenda that provides primary emphasis on those information areas that are most likely to prove productive in your networking meeting.

Best Time and Places for Networking Meetings

When planning the timing of a networking meeting it is a good idea to select a time of day when the networking contact is least likely to have time constraints. For example:

1. Late in the morning (11:00 a.m.), just before lunch (especially if you incorporate lunch as part of the meeting)
2. Late in day (4:00 p.m.), when the contact is least likely to have meetings scheduled afterward
3. Early morning breakfast meetings (7:00 a.m. or earlier)
4. Over dinner

By paying attention to the timing of your meeting, it is less likely that your networking contact will feel pressured to end the meeting.

This, of course, is to your benefit since it will allow the contact to relax and expand at greater length on those areas of greatest importance to you.

Whenever possible, it is a good idea to schedule networking meetings at places other than the networking contact's office. This is why meeting for breakfast, lunch, or dinner can often be more productive; they get the contact away from the office in a more neutral setting, and ensure that you have your contact's undivided attention. Meeting outside the office eliminates the possibility of business phone calls, visits from co-workers and other unwanted interruptions that can interfere with your networking discussion.

Of course you need to be accommodating to the needs of your networking contacts when arranging these meetings. If your contact is on a very tight schedule and the only time he or she can meet is Tuesday morning at 8:00 a.m. at the office, then by all means be there at that time! When you have options, however, try to schedule these meetings at a time and place where there will be sufficient time to discuss your job search and where interruptions will be held to an absolute minimum.

What to Take to the Meeting

Don't go to a networking meeting with the entire contents of your briefcase to unload on your networking contact. Believe me, this will not be appreciated. Leave your college transcripts, award certificates, trophies, last 10 performance evaluations, letters of recognition, and other such memorabilia at home. You don't want to overwhelm your newly found contact with a lot of detail. The rule is: Keep it simple and take only the following basic necessities along to your networking meeting:

1. Half a-dozen copies of your resume
2. Typewritten list of references
3. Leather-bound folder with tablet (for note taking)
4. A pen

If you are an artist or draftsperson, you may want to take sample drawings that illustrate your work. This is the exception to the rule, however, and is certainly not intended to suggest that others take work samples to the networking meeting as well. This is definitely not the case!

Do not automatically hand all six copies of your resume to your networking contact. Start by presenting your guest with a single copy of your resume for discussion purposes. If, later in the conversation, your contact offers to discuss your background with others, you may want to offer him or her the additional resume copies to facilitate such discussions. Otherwise, unless asked for additional copies, keep them in your folder and take them back home with you.

Likewise, don't automatically offer a copy of your list of references unless there is good reason to do so. In most cases, this is premature and inappropriate. Should your contact feel that he or she requires references, he or she will ask you for them.

What to Wear

Being appropriately dressed sends a positive message to your networking contact and makes him or her feel more comfortable about sharing the kinds of information and contacts that will be crucial to the success of your networking effort and, therefore, your job-hunting campaign.

As styles change, and more and more companies are adopting relaxed dress code standards, it is becoming more difficult to determine what appropriate dress is. Probably the best piece of advice is to wear what you expect your contact to be wearing.

If the site of your meeting is the corporate headquarters, and the norm is traditional single-breast gray or navy suits and white shirts with subtle patterned silk ties *or* classically styled one-or two-piece dresses with long sleeves and a navy, gray, or black jacket, then you'll want to dress accordingly. On the other hand, if the meeting site is a manufacturing plant and your guest is likely to be wearing jeans or a blue work uniform, you will not want to be overdressed. In this case, more casual clothes are appropriate.

It is a good rule to determine the dress code before your meeting so you are appropriately dressed. If this is not possible, then a good rule to follow is to dress more conservatively, as you would do for an employment interview. For men, this usually means a traditional single-breast gray or navy suit with a white shirt and all-silk tie with either a subtle pattern or stripe. For women, this normally means either a classic cut gray, navy, or black well-tailored suit *or* a classic styled, long-sleeved, one-or two-piece dress in navy, gray or black with an appropriate dress jacket. In all cases your clothing should be clean and neatly pressed. You should also be well-groomed and void of any fancy or gaudy jewelry. Also, avoid any bright or loud colors that might offend your guest.

Personal Presentation

The networking meeting is very similar to the employment interview. How you look and behave during the course of your presentation can have a very significant effect on the outcome of the networking meeting. Your presentation, both verbal and nonverbal, should create a favorable impression on your networking contact, right from the start, so that he or she will be motivated to help you be successful in your job search. There are three main elements to personal presentation. These are:

1. Body language
2. Presentation style
3. Communications skills

Body Language

There has been much written on the topic of body language as an important element in effective presentations. The position and use of your body can have a powerful influence on how others feel about you and their interpretation of the kind of person you are. For example, a person who slouches way down in a chair and looks at the floor while talking to others can present a very negative impression. This powerful form of nonverbal communication may suggest that such person is "lazy, poorly motivated, and lacking in self-confidence." By contrast, someone who sits "ramrod straight," is perched on the very edge of the chair, and continuously plays with a pencil throughout the conversation, may give a very different impression. Such body language may telegraph that this is an uptight, high-strung, and nervous person.

Thus, body language is a powerful nonverbal communicator, and needs to be something of which you are very conscious during the course of your networking meeting. Here are some basic guidelines for exhibiting good body language that are important to creating a positive impression.

- Exhibit good posture throughout your networking meeting.
- Sit reasonably erect (but not rigid) in your chair. (This suggests you have high energy, are well-motivated, attentive, and interested)
- Avoid slouching or assuming an overly rigid posture.
- Maintain good eye contact, but avoid staring.

- Avoid nervous distractions such as pencil tapping, playing with your hair, and pulling your ear.

- Make appropriate use of your hands (such as gesturing) to add emphasis to key points you are making and put more animation and energy into your overall presentation.

Presentation Style

Your presentation style needs to exhibit energy and enthusiasm for the topics under discussion. Demonstrate your interest in your networking contact by being a very attentive listener and reinforcing key points the person has made with appropriate commentary.

Exhibit a warm, friendly, open style that encourages your guest to feel relaxed and at-home in your company. This persuades your contact to open up with you and enable him or her to feel comfortable sharing such things as key contacts and sensitive information that may be particularly helpful to you. An occasional warm smile and nod of the head, at appropriate times, will go a long way toward establishing a less formal environment and enhancing personal rapport.

Communication Skills

In order to create a favorable impression and build the kind of relationship that is conducive to a successful networking meeting, you need to pay particular attention to your communications skills. The following should be characteristic of the way in which you communicate:

- Be expressive (use alive, animated speech).
- Be articulate (pronounce words clearly).
- Be concise (avoid being too wordy, rambling).
- Be focused (be exact, to the point).
- Be direct (be straightforward, not evasive).

Effective communication is critical to your overall personal presentation and the impression that you will have on your networking contact. The above communications guidelines will go a long way toward helping you create the kind of positive impression needed for effective networking.

Using the Indirect Versus Direct Approach

The general approach to the networking meeting is pretty much identical to the networking telephone call. You should use a softer more indirect approach when requesting assistance from your networking contact. Specifically, you want to avoid asking your networking contact directly for jobs or job leads. Since jobs and job leads are usually not something your contact can provide on an immediate basis, such "directness" can cause a sense of awkwardness and embarrassment and can get in the way of building the kind of personal rapport that is so essential to a productive networking discussion. Instead, make use of the indirect approach by asking your contact for things he or she can deliver. This normally means asking for information, ideas, and/or advice, all of which most networking contacts are more than happy to provide.

Chapter 5 provides a very thorough discussion of the indirect networking approach you might want to review it before proceeding with the balance of this chapter. Much of what is presented in chapter 5 on networking telephone calls applies equally well to conducting an effective networking meeting. It's important, therefore, for you to have a thorough grasp of these networking strategies and techniques before continuing with this chapter.

Critical Elements of the Networking Meeting

There are eight basic steps or components important to successful networking meetings:

- The greeting
- Small talk
- Appreciation statement
- Resume presentation
- Background summary (two-minute drill)
- Primary and secondary agenda
- Referrals
- Closing statement

These critical elements are illustrated in Figure 6.2 and are very similar to the fundamental elements of the networking call (see Figure 5.2) with a few exceptions. When reviewing Figure 6.2, notice that there is a logical flow or sequence to the order in which these topics are presented. This sequence represents the natural order in which these elements normally occur during the course of a typical networking meeting discussion. Let's now explore each of these meeting components in more detail.

CRITICAL ELEMENTS OF NETWORKING MEETING

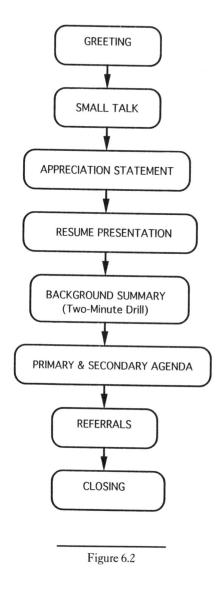

Figure 6.2

The Greeting

The first step to the networking meeting is the greeting. Although greeting content is pretty basic, the initial impression you create during your introduction will be very important to how well you will be received, and how willing your contact will be to provide meaningful assistance. So, make your greeting a good one!

Your greeting does much to set the stage for the tone of your meeting. It is important, therefore, that you are warm, friendly, and cordial during your introduction. This sets the stage for a more relaxed, friendly, and open discussion that encourages your contact to be more forthcoming in sharing ideas and information with you.

When greeting your contact, then, try to avoid appearing overly stiff or formal. A friendly smile, firm handshake, and some pleasant small talk, will usually go a long way to setting a proper mood for your conversation. Your greeting statement should be positive and upbeat and reflect a sense of positive energy that telegraphs to your contact that you are energized and enthusiastic about being there. You words and tone need to convey a sense of positive anticipation. Here are some typical greeting statements that might be used to set the stage for your meeting:

Example A

> *"Good morning, Dick, I'm Doug Baxter. I am really pleased to meet you and have been looking forward to our discussion. I certainly appreciate your willingness to meet with me on such short notice!"*

Example B

> *"Hello, Jane, I'm Jim Dawson. I'm so pleased to have this opportunity to meet with you. Joan has told me so much about you—all of which, I might add, has been very favorable. Thanks so much for agreeing to meet with me!"*

Notice a sense of enthusiasm and positive energy in each of the above examples. Can you feel the expression of appreciation for the meeting? Since your contact has obviously gone out of his or her way to meet with you, a brief thank-you during the greeting is certainly in order and will win a lot of points with your contact.

Small Talk

As with the networking phone call, the purpose of small talk is to set a more informal, relaxed tone for the conversation that is about to follow. Setting a conversational tone at the beginning of your discussion will be conducive to a more open, freer exchange of information. Often, it breaks down and removes many of the artificial social defense mechanisms that can so frequently get in the way of full, open communication.

The subjects chosen for small talk can cover a myriad of topics, too numerous to capture here. Try, whenever possible, to select a topic of mutual interest that will create a sense of "sharing." For example, if you know your contact is an avid sailor and you enjoy sailing as well, you might want to choose sailing as your topic:

Example:

Networker   *"I understand from Joanne that you are the proud skipper of a 38 foot Endeavor, and sail the upper reaches of the Chesapeake. The Endeavor has always been one of my favorites. How do you like her?"*

Another good topic for small talk is your referral source (the person who made the introduction to this contact). Since this relationship forms the basis for mutual commonality with your guest, it is normally an excellent choice for small talk. It also has the advantage of helping to cement a sense of common bond and frequently serves to enhance the contact's motivation to be helpful.

To prepare appropriately for small talk, call your referral source in advance of your networking meeting to thank him or her for the introduction and to confirm the forthcoming get-together. Your referral source will appreciate your thoughtfulness, and this conversation provides the perfect opportunity to learn more about your networking contact, including:

- The basis of your relationship with your referral source
- Extracurricular activities
- Unusual hobbies
- Personality profile
- Likes and dislikes

If you know your referral source well, you might also use this opportunity to ask for a little "friendly coaching" on how to best approach your networking contact during the forthcoming meeting. Your referral source might offer to pass along a personal message of some sort to your new networking contact (such as "Jim said to say hello, and also said to tell you that he is ready to get out on the links whenever you are"). You could prompt this possibility by simply asking your referral source if he or she would like you to pass along a message of any kind to the networking contact.

As you can see, small talk can be very beneficial to setting the right tone for your meeting, and there are any number of topics that could serve your purpose. If all else fails, however, and your referral source is simply not close enough to the networking contact to provide anything of substance for use in your small talk strategy, you might consider a more immediate, spontaneous approach using any of the following old standby topics:

- The weather
- Your surroundings
- An attractive article of clothing your contact is wearing
- General office decor
- A specific item in the office or restaurant (family picture, trophy, award plaque, painting, etc.)

Be alert to your surroundings and pick an item of personal nature for some brief small talk discussion. Things like a family portrait of personal awards are ideal for this purpose. They provide the opportunity for your contact to share some aspect of his or her personal life with you, which normally helps to establish that friendly, informal meeting setting you seek. Here are some examples of how the small talk technique can be used to help set the stage:

Example A

"Pete, you certainly have a great view of the Hudson from here! Do you ever find it distracting?"

Example B

> *"I'm glad that we are having the opportunity to have lunch here at Leonardi's. I've always heard great things about the food, and have always wanted to eat here. Have you been here before?"*

Example C

> *"Sandra tells me that you have a nice collection of art, including several Scarsborough originals. I've always liked Scarsborough. Have you been collecting his paintings for long?"*

Appreciation Statement

The appreciation statement is a transition statement that is used to gracefully transition the conversation from small talk to the real purpose of your meeting. It also serves the very practical purpose of letting your contact know, once again, how much you appreciate the time the person took to meet with you. It is used as a natural bridge that leads to the presentation of your resume to the contact. The following are very typical examples of well-positioned appreciation statements.

Example A

> *" Cordelia, I want to again express my appreciation for your meeting with me. Joan speaks so highly of you, and I was very much looking forward to our meeting."*

Example B

> *"John, I want to again let you know how much I appreciate your willingness to meet with me. I have been looking forward to meeting with you, and very much appreciate this opportunity. Thank you."*

Resume Presentation

At this point in the networking conversation, it is a good idea to get your resume into the hands of the networking contact, so he or she has a clearer picture of your overall experience and qualifications. Such overview of your qualifications is essential to the contact's understanding of your capabilities, and thereby facilitates a more focused and meaningful discussion. The technique to accomplish this is very simple. You simply hand the contact a copy of your resume and use commentary similar to the following:

Example A

> *(Hand resume to contact.) "Barb, I have brought along a copy of my resume to give you a more complete understanding of my background. Perhaps a good place to start would be for me to provide you with a brief overview of my qualifications and interests."*

Example B

> *(Hand resume to contact.) "Perhaps a good place to begin, Darwin, would be to provide you with a thumbnail sketch of my qualifications and interests. I brought along a copy of my resume for this purpose."*

This type of wording nicely sets the stage for you to present a brief synopsis of your background (commonly known in outplacement consulting circles as the two-minute drill).

Background Summary (The Two-Minute Drill)

The background summary or two-minute drill, as presented at this stage of your networking meeting, is intended to provide your contact with just enough information about your background and career interests to enable them to make appropriate recommendations to you. This summary needs to be brief, concise, and to the point.

The two-minute drill idea, as described in chapter 5, is intended to keep your presentation of your background summary to two minutes or less. If you force yourself to stay within this two-minute parameter, you will tend to present your contacts with just enough information to facilitate a meaningful networking discussion, but not too much information that will bore them.

Generally, this background description includes your educational credentials, jobs you have held, companies for whom you have worked, and a brief summary of some of your key strengths and/or accomplishments. It should also include a brief description of the type of position you are seeking. Examples of some typical background summary statements follow. You should use these to develop similar summaries for use in your networking meeting.

Example A

"Kay, I am a 1975 graduate of Lehigh University where I earned a bachelor's degree in Mechanical Engineering. I followed this with an M.B.A. from the Wharton School in 1981. I initially began my career as a project engineer with Air Products in their Industrial Gasses Division. This entailed the design and construction of on-site customer storage and delivery facilities. I left Air Products in 1982 to accept the position of Project Engineering Manager for Dow Chemical's Specialty Chemicals Division in Midland, Michigan, where I was responsible for the design, installation, and start-up of major chemical manufacturing facilities throughout the United States. I have managed large-scale capital projects, including the engineering of complete chemical plants. Some of these were in excess of $100 million and necessitated managing teams of up to 100 engineers. In 1994 I was promoted to senior engineering manager. As you can see, my strength is in successfully managing the engineering of large-scale capital projects in the chemical industry, and I am now looking for a senior level executive position in a similar setting."

Example B

"Ellen, to save you the time of reading my resume, let me take a minute or two to provide you with a quick summary of my background. I graduated in 1982 with a bachelor's degree in Accounting from Ohio State. I began my career as a manufacturing cost accountant with Meade Paper Company at their manufacturing site in Red Bank, Ohio. I became manager of cost accounting at that site in 1986, and was then promoted to mill controller two years later, in 1988. This assignment was followed by promotion to Controller of the Company's Coated Papers Division in 1992, which is my current position. In this position I am responsible for all accounting functions for a five plant, $1.4 billion operation and manage an accounting staff of 14 professionals. I am now interested in returning to the East Coast, and am looking for a position as a division or corporate controller with a major manufacturing company."

Primary and Secondary Agenda

Having provided your contact with an understanding of your qualifications and career interests, it is now time to skillfully focus conversation on the primary and secondary agendas you have established on your meeting planning form (see Figure 6.1). Following presentation of your two-minute, you need to immediately transition to conversation in these specific areas, starting with those topics (or requests) that you have established as your primary agenda.

Remember, you do not want to scare your guest off by being too direct. Specifically, you do not want to ask for key contacts or job leads at this juncture. To do so will likely cause your contact some nervousness and he or she may "clam up" on you. It is simply too soon in the conversation for these topics. Wait until you have made it through the social warm-up period and have established a bit more personal rapport prior to popping these more sensitive questions.

Instead, focus on using the indirect approach. Keep your initial questions to requests for advice, ideas, general information, observations, and the like. As discussed in chapter 5, these are the deliverables—the pieces of information most contacts are most able and willing to provide. Asking for such items as key contacts or job leads at this point in the conversation may cause your contact to "head for the tall timbers" in a hurry. Asking for these things prematurely could cause awkwardness or embarrassment (especially if your contact cannot immediately think of key contacts or job leads), in which case your contact may start looking for excuses to end your meeting early. Some of the safer areas to exploit at this point in your conversation include:

- General job-hunting advice
- Ideas on general job-hunting strategy
- Ideas on good job-hunting sources
- Ideas on good job-hunting techniques
- General observations about your target industry
- Observations about current target industry trends or events that might influence your job search

The idea is to start with broad, easier topics that will get your contact talking and accustomed to the idea of helping you. Then, as conversation continues and your personal rapport grows, gradually transition to the tougher and more sensitive topics such as requests for key contacts and job leads. If you have done a good job with your networking conversation, by then your contact will feel more relaxed and be far more inclined to address these important areas in a more meaningful way.

The following are examples of key warm-up questions that can be employed early in this stage of the conversation:

Example A

"Craig, as you think about the current state of the steel industry, what trends and/or events do you see having the greatest impact on my job search? What recommendations do you have?"

Example B

"In light of my background and career interests, Sally, what thoughts or ideas do you have about effective job-hunting strategy? Are there specific thought or ideas that you could share with me?"

From these examples, you can readily see how easy it is to ask broad, sweeping questions and still get your contact person focused on the idea of helping you with your job search. You would be well advised, in advance of your networking meeting, to formulate similar type lead-in questions, so that you are not fumbling around for just the right question to ask at this crucial moment in the networking discussion. One or too well-formulated questions will certainly get you off to the right start and contribute significantly to the overall success of your networking effort. Don't take a chance by waiting until you get there. Have these lead-in questions ready to go, right from the start.

Referrals

Once the conversation is going smoothly, you feel you have successfully negotiated the social warm-up period, and you have established sufficient personal rapport with your networking contact, it is time to approach those more difficult questions. Here again, don't leave the framing of these important questions to chance. Make sure that you have both planned and practiced these questions in advance so the transition will go smoothly and naturally. By doing this, you increase your personal comfort level with these topics and are far more effective at getting the kind of information you need .

Once again, avoid asking for jobs and job leads during your net-working discussion. If you follow the strategy outlined in this book and thereby establish sufficient rapport with your networking contact, your contact will volunteer job leads, and you will never have to ask for them.

So, at this juncture (assuming you have concluded discussion of the more general issues), it is time to ask for the names of key contacts and referrals.

These are the lifeline of the networking process and *must* be devel-oped if your networking effort is to remain alive and healthy. Here are some ways of requesting such referrals that are particularly effective:

Example A

"As you know, Jim, in this tight labor market networking plays a critical role in finding employment. I'm sure you can appre-ciate, therefore, the importance of continuously developing meaningful contacts. Jim, as you think about the people whom you know in the industry—especially those who are well con-nected and seem to know a lot of others—who are some of the people whom you believe it would be good for me to contact?"

Example B

"Carol, who are some of the key people you could recommend, for networking purposes, who appear to be well connected and know a lot of other people in the industry? Perhaps some of the vendors you have dealt with, people met at association meet-ings, consultants or others who have a number of contacts and knowledge of the industry."

Example C

"Walt, if you were in my shoes, who are some of the people who are associated with the industry, and with whom you would want to be in contact? I'm thinking about such people as ven-dors, consultants, association officers, key industry leaders, or any others who are well connected and seem to know what's going on."

Don't forget, once you have been given the name of a new contact, you need to acquire two additional pieces of information from your refer-ral source:

1. The nature of the referral source's relationship with the new contact (how they know one-another)
2. Permission to use the referral source's name when introducing yourself to the new contact

Understanding the nature of the relationship will give you some basis for formulating effective small talk during your subsequent phone call to the new contact. Use of the referral source's name, when introducing yourself to this new contact, will heighten the contact's sense of obligation to respond to you in an appropriate and meaningful way. Sample techniques for your use in clarifying the relationship between your source and the new contact follow:

Example A

"How did you get to know Bertha?"

Example B

"Do you know Dave well?"

Techniques you can use to get permission from your referral source to use his or her name when introducing yourself to the new networking contact are:

Example A

"Deborah, would you mind if I mentioned to Don that you suggested I give him a call?"

Example B

"May I tell June that you suggested I call?"

Closing

Once you have concluded your networking discussion and achieved the objectives that you established for your meeting, it is time for the close.

The networking close has four basic components:

1. The appreciation statement
2. The additional ideas and contacts statement
3. The future follow-up statement

4. The final thank-you statement

The following sample closing statement incorporates each of the above elements. The numbers enclosed in parenthesis enable you to distinguish each of these key components (see number coding in above listing) and see how they are used.

Example

(1) "Listen, Bill, I want to thank you for meeting with me today. This was a very enlightening and helpful conversation, and I really appreciate the time you have spent with me. (2) If, over the next couple of days, you have any other ideas you believe would be helpful to me, or if you think of others with whom I should be in contact, I would very much appreciate hearing from you. My phone number is, of course, on my resume. (3) Likewise, I plan to stay in touch and keep you abreast of my progress from time to time. (4) Again, Bill, I really appreciate your help. Thank you!"

The Follow-up Thank You Letter

When someone has been kind enough to take personal time to meet with you, basic courtesy dictates that you follow your networking meeting with an appropriate thank you letter. Common courtesy also dictates that you call the person, from time to time, to let him or her know how you are doing and to provide your contact with feedback on the results of his or her suggestions and referrals.

These are valuable contacts with whom you will want to stay in touch and whose friendships you will want to continue to cultivate long after your job search has been successfully concluded. Stay in touch with these people, calling them from time to time to simply say hello, and always offering to help them in any way you can. You never know when you will need them again, and perhaps there will be a time when you can return their kindness. Figure 6.3 is a sample follow-up thank you letter that should be helpful to you.

SAMPLE "THANK YOU" LETTER

1220 Winding Lane
Wallingford, PA 19872

January 22, 1995

Mr. David E. Jenkins
Director of Public Affairs
Baxter Company, Inc.
500 East High View Blvd.
Boston, MA 12665

Dear Dave:

Thank you very much for the time you spent with me on Monday. Knowing the hectic schedule you keep, I'm sure that stealing two hours away from the office to spend helping me was no easy matter. Hopefully, someday I will have the opportunity to return the kindness.

In particular, Dave, I appreciated the introductions to Sid Cressman and Joanne Wakefield. Both have agreed to meet with me, and I am looking forward to my sessions with them. Joanne, especially, seems to know a lot of key players in the food industry, and has been most gracious in her offers to assist me with some key introductions. I am meeting with her this coming Monday, and will let you know the outcome.

I also wish to thank you for your excellent recommendations for improving my resume. I have made the suggested changes, and am pleased to say that it now reads far more forcefully. The improvement stands in testimony to your excellent communications skills as a top-notch public affairs professional.

Thank you again, Dave, for your kindness and for spending the time with me. Your help and offer of continuing support are greatly appreciated.

Regards,

Steve

Steve Wileman

Figure 6.3

Chapter 7

Getting Past the Secretary/Gatekeeper

As a networker, unless you are prepared to effectively deal with the many barriers a skilled secretary can place in your way at the time of your networking call, you will never even get the opportunity to talk with your targeted contacts and your job search will be severely handicapped. Unfortunately, most job seekers are simply not sufficiently skilled at fielding these objections and therefore often allow the slightest resistance to become a major deterrent to reaching their job-search objectives.

Effective employment networking therefore requires that you anticipate most of these secretarial barriers in advance and learn how to gracefully overcome such obstacles before making your networking calls. It is important that you also employ counterstrategies and techniques that allow you to succeed in your networking objectives, yet still preserve and strengthen your relationship with this key person. How well you field these secretarial objections, and how you treat the secretary in the process, often prove to be critical factors in determining whether or not you reach your targeted networking contact.

Formulating solid strategies for successfully addressing these barriers and effectively managing secretarial relationships first begins with understanding and appreciating the roles secretaries play and the basic rules by which they operate in fulfilling their responsibilities to their boss. As long as you are courteous, respect their role, and operate within the basic rules of acceptable professional conduct, there is a good likelihood that the secretary will become a friendly ally in your attempt to reach his or her boss. Conversely, discourteous behavior, disregard for their roles, and/or violation of the basic rules of professional conduct are likely to cause unwanted animosity and result in your "remaining out in the cold."

Role of the Secretary

As we all know, one of the key roles of a valued secretary is the effective screening of incoming telephone calls. In this important role, the secretary serves as a gatekeeper—the first line of defense in filtering out those many unwanted telephone calls that the boss does not wish to receive. Managing the screening process is a function that is greatly appreciated by busy managers who simply cannot afford to waste time or be distracted by many details.

When fielding incoming phone calls, there appears to be a fairly universal protocol that is generally followed by most secretaries:

1. Determine the name of the person who is calling.
2. Ascertain the nature of caller's relationship to the boss.
3. Determine the purpose of the call.
4. Personally provide needed information (as appropriate).
5. Refer call to other people or departments (where warranted).
6. Take a message and offer to have the boss return the call (as appropriate).
7. Refer call directly to boss (where warranted).

Well-trained, efficient assistants are very protective of their bosses' time. They take seriously their role in screening the boss from unnecessary contacts and activities that could waste time and detract the boss from staying focused on important matters. In this way, they enable the boss to remain focused on only those activities that are truly important to job and career success. This is an invaluable service that most bosses greatly appreciate, and it is one to which you need be particularly sensitive.

Efficient secretaries are also well tuned-in to their bosses' schedules and work priorities. They are ever-mindful of the need to protect their boss during times of unusually heavy workload and tight deadlines. When the situation warrants, they will screen out certain telephone calls entirely. With other more sensitive calls, they are expected to exercise appropriate discretion and judgment when deciding which calls to put through and which to screen.

External Phone Calls

External phone calls are bound to receive far more attention and careful scrutiny by the conscientious secretary than those coming from within the organization, especially since a high percentage of such external calls are placed by vendors who wish to sell something to the boss. Unless carefully screened, these calls can prove very disruptive to a busy manager.

When your networking call is screened by the administrative assistant, therefore, you can fully expect that the assistant is going to be equally thorough in probing the reason for your call. As previously mentioned, the main thrust of his or her inquiry will likely be on getting answers to the following:

- Who is calling?
- What is the caller's relationship to the boss?
- What is purpose of the call?
- Does the caller have a legitimate reason or need to talk with the boss? Now? Later? Directly? Through secretary?

Knowing, in advance, that this is likely to be the gatekeeper's line of inquiry allows the networker to anticipate and prepare for these questions. How well prepared the networker is to provide meaningful answers will invariably have significant impact on the networker's ability to gain access to the targeted contact.

Thus, a good presentation during the introductory phase of the networking process is absolutely essential to success. To be effective, this introduction needs to accomplish three primary objectives:

1. Establish that there is a personal or professional connection with the boss

2. Establish the legitimate need to have direct conversation with the boss

3. Secure secretary's commitment to help you make contact with the boss

If you fail to accomplish any of these three goals during the initial stages of your conversation with the administrative assistant, you drastically decrease your chances of being put through to your contact.

The Basic Introduction

The basic introduction is fairly simplistic but, nonetheless, can often provide instant gratification to the job seeker. When using this approach, the networker simply introduces him or herself and then asks to speak with the targeted executive. Sometimes, this simple technique is all that is needed to blow right by the gatekeeper to the networking contact. The following are some examples of the basic introduction:

Example A
Networker   *"Good morning, is Karen Anders in please?"*

Secretary   *"Who is calling?"*

Networker   *"This is Dave Silver. Is Karen available?"*

Secretary   *"Just a moment, Mr. Silver, I will connect you."*

Networker   *"Thank you!"*

Example B
Networker   *"Good morning, this is Steve Jordan calling. May I speak with Mary Smith please?"*

Secretary   *"Yes, Steve. One moment please, and I'll connect you."*

Networker   *"Thank you!"*

Example C
Networker   *"Good afternoon, this is Cora Norton calling. With whom am I speaking?"*

Secretary   *"This is Bob Nelson."*

Networker   *"Bob, is Bill Johnston in please?"*

Secretary   *"Just a moment, Cora, I'll see."*

Networker   *"Thank you."*

All networking introductions should start with this basic approach. Begin with a simple greeting (such as "Good morning" or "Good afternoon"), followed by your name, and then a request to speak with your networking contact. When known, always refer to your networking contact by their first name rather than Mr. or Ms. This suggests to the secretary that you are a first name basis with their boss, which enhances the probability that you will get through the net.

This basic introduction approach subscribes to the theory, "Never volunteer more information than is absolutely necessary." If the gatekeeper doesn't ask any further questions, don't provide any additional information. At this stage of the game, this basic information is all that is necessary for the secretary to pass your call along to your targeted contact. Simply wait, then, until your contact is put on the line, and then proceed with your networking call strategy.

One key mistake inexperienced networkers frequently make is to prematurely volunteer information beyond that which has been requested by the administrative assistant. For example, they may volunteer why they are calling or may state the basis for their referral to the networking contact. Such additional information is unwarranted and may stimulate the secretary's curiosity, serving to prompt the gatekeeper to ask more probing questions concerning the legitimacy of the call.

As illustrated in example C, asking the assistant's name during the networking call introduction adds a nice personal touch to the conversation. The additional advantage of this tactic is that it places you on a first-name basis with the secretary in the event that your networking contact is not in, and you need to call back later. In such event, the assistant is likely to feel far more congenial and friendly if you show that you were considerate enough to remember his or her name from your initial conversation.

Target Contact not Available

What do you do when the gatekeeper advises you that your intended contact is not available? Do you leave a message for them to call you back? Or should you take the initiative by offering to call again later?

Knowledgeable job-search experts seem to uniformly agree on the answer to this one: offer to call back later at a time convenient to your contact. Unless asked, however, avoid disclosing to the secretary (or answering machine) the reason for your call. (If an answering machine or voice mail, simply leave your name, phone number, and a simple request that your contact return your call.)

Here are some sample dialogues that illustrate how to properly handle this networking obstacle.

Example A

Secretary   *"I'm sorry but Mr. Jackson isn't in. Would you like to leave a message?"*

Networker   *"Thank you, but it will probably be easier for me to call back. When would be a good time to reach him?"*

Secretary   *"It's hard to say—he has such a busy schedule. He usually comes in early and is at his desk around 7:30 a.m., however. You might try then."*

Networker   *"Thanks, Sandra, I'll give it a try then."*

Secretary   *"Your welcome, John. I'll alert him to expect your call."*

Example B

Secretary   *"I'm sorry, but Ms. Faulk is on vacation this week."*

Networker   *"I see. When do you expect her to return, Barbara?"*

Secretary   *"Well, she's not due back in until next Wednesday, but it looks like she'll be in meetings all day Wednesday and Thursday and will be hard to reach."*

Networker   *"When do you feel would be a good time to try to reach her?"*

Secretary   *"I would try sometime after 2:00 p.m. on the following Monday. It looks like the dust will have settled by then."*

Networker   *"Thanks, Barbara, I'll plan to call her on Monday."*

Secretary   *"You're quite welcome, Dick."*

Example C

Secretary   *"I'm sorry, Susan, but Mr. Jones is in a meeting at the moment and can't be reached. Would you like me to have him return your call?"*

Networker   *"Thank you, Linda, but it will probably difficult for him to reach me. Why don't I plan to call back later. Is there a time that would be good to try to reach Bob?"*

Secretary   *"You might try on Wednesday at about 1:15 p.m. He should have returned from lunch by then, and doesn't have any meetings scheduled until 2:00 p.m."*

Networker   *"Great, I'll try to reach him then. Thank you, Linda."*

Secretary   *"You're welcome, Susan."*

These sample networking dialogues reveal the application of certain fundamental principles when you are told by the administrative assistant that your networking target is unavailable. These are simply:

- Don't request that the contact return your call.
- Instead, offer to call back at a convenient time.
- Determine the best time to call.

You may be wondering what the logic behind this line of reasoning is. First, by following these guidelines you always keep control of the process, and don't let the process control you. As soon as you leave a message for the contact to return your call, you forfeit control of the process. Your networking success is now totally dependent upon this return phone call, and it just might not happen!

Should the target contact not return your call, you have lost valuable job-search time. You are also now forced to call a second time, despite the fact protocol dictates you await return of your initial phone call. Besides the feelings of degradation associated with making this second call, there is also the risk that you may now be perceived as impatient, a pest,—or both! Additionally, when you do call your networking contact back this second time, you still have no idea whether or not this person will be available. If again unavailable, this call will now trigger a third call and further delay your networking effort. When this scenario is multiplied by several similar situations, the negative impact on your overall job-search can be quite significant. It can cumulatively add significant delay and the possibility of several unwanted months to your job search effort.

An additional major disadvantage to leaving a message for the networking contact to return your call, is that this return call may come at an inconvenient time—a time when you are least prepared to handle it. Obviously, this can be unsettling and further handicap your networking efforts. By contrast, if you offer to make these return calls, you remain in control of the process and are likely to be far more effective in that you will know just exactly what it is you want to accomplish and say. In this way both confidence and effectiveness are greatly enhanced, as is networking success.

Finally, if you are on another call at the time your target contact does call back, there will be further delays to the networking process. You may now become engaged in a game of "telephone tag" that could go on indefinitely. This could result in numerous calls until contact is finally made. Additionally, with each subsequent call back, you increase the likelihood that the secretary may ask more questions and screen you out before you have successfully established contact with the boss.

Thus, as you can see, it is to your best advantage to tell the secretary that you will call back, and fully utilize the secretary's knowledge of the boss's schedule to establish the best time for this call back. This way you substantially reduce the number of phone calls required to reach your contact, and you are far better prepared to handle the call once contact has been made.

Level 1 Objection—Your Relationship With Boss

In the previous discussion of the basic introduction, the assumption was made that the assistant would simply put the call through to his or her boss without further qualifying the legitimacy of the call. This is seldom the case.

More often than not, the secretary screens your call more thoroughly than this. In doing so, he or she first tries to establish two key pieces of information—who you are and the nature of your relationship with the boss. In order to be effective in your networking efforts, therefore, you need to be able to answer these questions in such a way as to encourage the secretary to put your call through or, if the boss is not there, to offer to assist you in making contact.

In attempting to establish your identity, as well as relationship to the gatekeeper's boss, most secretaries are well equipped with several probing questions designed to accomplish this:

- Is Mr. Jones expecting your call?
- Will Mr. Jones know what this call is in reference to?
- Does Mr. Jones know you personally?
- Will Mr. Jones recognize your name?

The following networking dialogues illustrate the use of these questions by the secretary and suggest ways that you might successfully handle them.

Example A

Secretary   *"Is Mr. Jones expecting your call?"*

Networker   *"No, but please tell him I was referred to him by June Halston."*

Secretary   *"I see. Just a moment, Melinda, I'll see if he can take your call."*

Networker   *"Thank you."*

Example B

Secretary   *"Will Ms. Martin know what this call is in reference to?"*

Networker   *"No, but please tell her that I am calling at the suggestion of Bill Marsden."*

Secretary   *"Okay. Just a moment and I'll see if she can take your call."*

Networker   *"Thank you very much."*

Example C

Secretary   *"Does Mr. Thornton know you personally?"*

Networker   *"No, but I was referred by Jan Wilson, a friend of his."*

Secretary   *"I see. Well, let me see if I can find him. I know he's in the area."*

Networker   *"Thank you, Sandra, I appreciate that."*

Example D

Secretary   *"Will Linda recognize your name?"*

Networker   *"I don't believe so, but please tell her that Dorothy Lang suggested I contact her."*

Secretary   *"One moment, John. Let me see if I can get her on the line."*

Networker   *"Thank you, Judy."*

As you can see from these examples, the key to successfully handling level 1 objections is to use the name of your referral as the basis for establishing the relationship with the boss. Simply mentioning the referral's name, and stating that you were referred by this person, suggests to the secretary that you are well connected and therefore have a legitimate reason to speak with the boss.

Again, it is that sense of personal or professional obligation to respond, resulting from personal referral, that holds the networking process together and makes it work. The mere mention of the referral's name to the secretary suggests that the boss has some kind of relationship with the referring source and there is an obligation to talk with you.

Since the secretary has no means of assessing the extent of this relationship, he or she will normally opt to play it safe by assuming that the relationship between the referring source and the boss is a close one. Few secretaries will willingly accept the risk of challenging the nature of the relationship by asking additional questions. To do so borders on being intrusive and socially inappropriate. Most secretaries are unwilling to accept this added risk and will therefore simply pass your call along to the boss.

Level 2 Objection—Nature of Your Call

Those assistants who are particularly assertive and self-confident may be willing to take things to the next step. They are not so easily intimidated by the caller and, despite the mention of a referral's name, insist on knowing the reason for your call before they agree to place you in contact with the boss. This is what I call a level 2 objection.

When calls are screened this tightly, you know you are dealing with a real pro. The four common objectives to be served by this additional level of screening are:

- To screen out unnecessary, unwanted calls
- To save the boss time
- To allow the secretary to provide needed information (instead of bothering the boss)
- To redirect calls elsewhere, when they can be better handled by another function or individual.

The seasoned gatekeeper, who is determined to conserve the manager's time, can make employment networking an increasingly difficult task for the job seeker. The following represent a few ways that secretaries may elect to word level 2 objections when attempting to further screen networking calls:

- What is the nature of your call, Mr. Randolph?
- May I advise Ms. Figgins why you are calling?
- May I ask what your call is in reference to, Ms. Foster?
- Mr. Perkins, may I inquire whether this call is of a personal or business nature?
- What do you wish to discuss with Ms. Dunkin?
- Will Mr. Davis know why you are calling?
- Why are you calling, Ms. Wilkins?

The following are a few select sample networking calls that may give you some ideas on how to effectively field this type of objection:

Example A

Secretary *"What is the nature of your call, Mr. Randolph?"*

Networker *"I am calling at the suggestion of Sandra Jones to ask John's advice on a personal matter."*

Secretary *"I see. Let me see if he is in his office."*

Networker *"Thank you, Mary."*

Example B

Secretary *"May I ask what this call is in reference to, Dave?"*

Networker *"Yes, Linda, Jim Parker seemed to feel Alex could help me with a personal matter."*

Secretary *"Would you mind being more specific?"*

Networker *"No. I am in the process of a career transition, and Jim seemed to feel that Alex would be an excellent person to talk with concerning his general thoughts and ideas on job-hunting strategy. Please tell him I only need a few minutes of his time, and that I am not expecting him to be aware of a job for me. I am only seeking his advice, and would appreciate the opportunity to talk with him."*

Secretary *"Let me see what I can do."*

Networker *"Thank you, Linda."*

Example C

Secretary *"Will Mr. Davis know why you are calling?"*

Networker *"No, but please tell him that Dorris Burger suggested I call."*

Secretary *"May I ask what you wish to discuss with Mr. Davis?"*

Networker *"Certainly. Dorris seemed to feel John would be a good person from whom to seek advice on a personal matter."*

Secretary *"I see. May I ask the nature of this personal matter?"*

Networker *"Of course. I am in the process of a career change and would very much appreciate his general counsel and advice."*

Secretary *"Okay, Betty. Let me see if Mr. Davis is free to take your call."*

Example D

Secretary *"Phyliss, is this call of a personal or business nature?"*

Networker *"Basically, it is personal in nature."*

Secretary *"May I advise Ms. Walters of the subject?"*

Networker *"Yes, please tell her that I am calling for some general counsel concerning my career. Sylvia Pates seemed to feel Kathy would be an excellent person to speak with on this subject."*

Secretary *"Let me check with Ms. Walters to see if she can take your call."*

Networker *"Thank you."*

Example E

Secretary *"Mr. Johns is very busy at the moment. May I ask why you are calling?"*

Networker *"Yes, I am calling at the suggestion of Walt Pearson. Walt said that Dave would be an excellent person to consult concerning the overall status of the fasteners industry. I am in the process of a career change, and have targeted the fasteners industry. I would certainly appreciate his overall observations and ideas. I would be pleased to call back at another time, however, if this is not a convenient time for Dave to talk."*

Secretary *"Let me check."*

Networker *"I appreciate your help, Rhonda, Thank you."*

When initially asked by the secretary why are calling, your first response should be that you are calling at the suggestion of your referral source to seek the target contact's advice on a "personal matter." The fact that you state it is with regard to a personal matter will frequently cause most secretaries to back off and put the call through to their superior without further screening.

In the preceding examples, the legitimacy of your need to talk with the boss is further reinforced through use of the name of the referral source. When told the caller has been referred by an acquaintance of the boss, and is calling regarding a personal matter, most assistants offer little or any further resistance, and will put the caller in touch with their boss.

However, not all secretaries are satisfied with the explanation that you are calling with regard to a personal matter. Some of the more persistent gatekeepers insist on knowing more about the reason for your call before they agree to put you in contact with their boss. They insist on knowing the specific reason why you are calling.

When this happens, it's time to come clean. There is no point in beating around the bush any further. Doing so often risks alienating the secretary—something you really don't want to do. At this stage, you are of course still very much dependent upon this individual as the key link with your networking contact. Getting this key person upset is clearly not going to be in your best interest.

So, when you are asked the second time to state the reason for your call, it is best to tell the assistant what he or she want to know. Explain to this person you are in the process of a "career transition" and that you are calling for their boss' general "counsel" and "advice." Make sure, however, that the secretary realizes that you will not be asking their boss for a job.

Use of the phrase "career transition" is rather benign. It raises few red flags since the secretary cannot tell whether or not you are still employed. Additionally, use of the words "ideas," "counsel," and "advice" usually relieve some of the anxiety that might otherwise be present if it were thought you were looking for either a job or job leads. It is this indirect approach (asking for "deliverables") that serves you far better than stating that the reason for your call is to look for a job.

Level 3 Objections—Stonewalling

Having survived both level 1 and level 2 objections does not mean that you are home scot-free. If you are up against a truly tenacious gatekeeper, you may still need to get through one additional level of objections if your networking effort is to survive.

At level 3, you can be hit with some of the toughest objections of all. At this point the secretary is engaged in what I call "stonewalling." Objections falling into this category appear almost impossible to counter. The nature of these objections makes it crystal clear that the secretary has absolutely no intention of allowing you to contact the boss. This is networking at its toughest. The following are examples of several of the more common stonewalling objections that comprise the secretarial arsenal:

- Ms. Dixon doesn't take calls of this type.
- You need to talk with Human Resources; they handle all employment matters.

- Send us your resume and I'll be glad to have Ms. Devereau review it.
- Company policy does not permit employees to accept personal calls.
- Linda prefers not to provide job-hunting assistance.
- I'm sorry, but Mr. Dixon is simply too busy to take your call.
- Ms. Stevens has suggested you contact Jan Higgins in our employment department.

Although these are truly tough objections to tackle, your success as a networker is dependent upon your ability to penetrate these remaining obstacles. This is certainly no time to roll over and play dead!

Let's take each of these objections, one at a time, and see how they might best be handled through sample dialogue that illustrates a good countertactic:

Example A: The Boss Doesn't Take Calls of This Type

Secretary *"I'm sorry, Cindy, but Mr. Russell doesn't take calls of this type."*

Networker *"Wilma, can you be more specific? What kind of calls doesn't Keith take?"*

Secretary *"Yes, he doesn't take employment inquiries."*

Networker *"I can appreciate that, Wilma, however, I am not really inquiring about opportunities for employment with your company. I am calling at Barb Wilson's suggestion to seek Keith's general advice and counsel. Barb speaks highly of his knowledge of the power industry and seems to feel he might be willing to share his general thoughts and observations with me. I would really appreciate his help."*

Secretary *"Just a moment, Cindy, I'll see if he will take your call."*

As you can see, this is a particularly difficult objection to handle, and it requires some assertiveness and persistence on your part. If you don't "push the envelope" on this one, however, you'll never talk to your target contact, and another good networking opportunity will have been lost. The counterstrategy for use in overcoming this particular obstacle is to ask the secretary to clarify what is meant by "calls of this type." simply ask for clarification of this terminology.

In more cases than not, the secretary means that the boss doesn't take inquiries directed at employment with the company. So, by making it clear that you are *not* seeking employment with the company, and by reframing your request to focus on your need for "general information and advice," there is a reasonable chance you will be successful in removing this barrier and reaching your networking contact. Reminding the secretary of the fact that you were referred by someone with whom his/her boss is acquainted also increases your chances of being put through.

Example B: You Need to Talk with Human Resources

Secretary   *"John, you need to talk with Hal Jones in Human Resources. Hal handles all employment matters for Vassar Corporation. Would you like me to transfer the call?"*

Networker   *"I would be glad to speak with Hal, but I'm not sure he can really help me. You see, Sally, I'm not really calling about employment opportunities with Vassar. I understand from Steve Larson that Karl has an excellent broad-based knowledge of the beverage industry, and would be a great person to talk with about current trends in bottling operations that might impact the direction of my career. I would really value his general counsel and observations, if he could spare a few minutes to speak with me."*

Secretary   *"I see, John. Let me see if Karl is available."*

As with the previous objection, the secretary has again made the assumption that the networker is seeking employment with the company. The automatic reaction then is to immediately refer the call to the employment department—a common practice of many secretaries when they feel the inquiry is employment related.

When countering this objection, it's important to make it clear to the secretary that you are *not* calling about employment with the company. This message can be further reinforced by explaining that, due to the specific technical nature of your inquiry, the employment department is unlikely to be able to help you. In doing this, you establish a legitimate need to speak directly with your targeted contact. You should also gently remind the secretary that you have been referred by someone who knows the boss, and that this referral source has strongly recommended you speak directly with the boss due to the boss's expert knowledge in this area. This strategy, combined with courtesy and a friendly demeanor, will often serve to get your call transferred to your networking contact.

Example C: Why Don't You Send Us Your Resume

Secretary *"Mr. Baxter is very busy right now. Joan, why don't you send him a copy of your resume for his review. I'll be glad to see that he gets it."*

Networker *"Thank you for the suggestion, Sandra, I appreciate your help. I'll plan to put a copy in the mail today. Perhaps I can call back in a week or so, however, when Bill's schedule is a little less hectic and he has a few moments to talk. I am told by Linda Snyderman that Bill is very active on the APPI Board, and would be an excellent person to talk with about some of the key technical trends in the pulp and paper industry. She feels he is particularly insightful and creative and might have some good ideas for me. I would really appreciate his counsel. When would be a good time to call back?"*

Secretary *"It's really hard to say, Joan, but why don't you call in the afternoon of the 15th. His schedule looks clean then."*

Networker *"Thank you, Sandra. I'll plan to call back on the 15th."*

When a secretary uses the "resume request tactic" as a barrier to completing contact with the boss, you should respond positively and courteously. Thank the secretary for the suggestion and offer to send the resume, as requested. However, you will want to quickly switch the focus of your conversation away from discussion of your resume to your desire to still have direct conversation with the boss. Acknowledge the boss' busy schedule, and then offer to call back at a more convenient time.

Try to establish when the best time would be for you to place this second call. In doing so, you are causing the secretary to take a positive step in facilitating future contact with the boss. This makes it more difficult for him or her to sidestep your request to speak with the boss at the time of this return call.

Notice the use of the referral's name as a further ploy for establishing the legitimacy of your request. Reminding the assistant that you were referred by someone who knows the boss helps establish that sense of professional or social need to respond. Since the secretary has no way of assessing the level or closeness of this relationship, there is a high likelihood that he or she will elect to play it safe, and put your second call through to your intended contact.

Example D: Company Policy Prohibits Personal Calls

Secretary   *"I'm sorry, Mary Sue, but company policy prohibits employees from taking personal calls during business hours."*

Networker   *"I'm sorry, Bill, I didn't know about your policy. Perhaps I could call Jim at his home in the evening. Do you happen to have his home number handy?"*

Secretary   *"I do. However, I can't give it to you without Jim's permission."*

Networker   *"Would you mind asking him if it would be all right? Please tell him that Randy Jones suggested I call him."*

Secretary   *"Just a minute, and I'll check with him."*

Networker   *"Thank you."*

Secretary   *"Jim says it is all right, and said to have you call after 7:30 p.m. His phone number is 433-9837."*

Networker   *"Thank you, Bill. I appreciate your help."*

Secretary   *"Your welcome."*

When confronted with a company policy that prohibits personal telephone calls (and there are a few companies with such policies), you want to acknowledge your acceptance of the policy and then offer to contact your target executive at home during nonbusiness hours. If you do not already have it, you want to remember to ask for the executive's home phone number, however, so that you will be able to make contact.

The secretary is usually not able to provide a home phone number from the person you are attempting to reach. In such cases, simply ask the secretary if he or she could request this approval from the contact. In most cases, due to the networking referral, the target contact gives permission and you are provided with the home phone number.

Example E: Prefers Not to Give Job-Hunting Assistance

Secretary   *"I'm sorry, Dick, but Michelle doesn't provide job hunting assistance."*

Networker   *"I see, Carolyn; however, please let Michelle know that I am not contacting her for a job or even job leads, for that matter. In fact, I am really not expecting this kind of assistance at all. What I am calling for, however, is some general advice and counsel. Althea said that Michelle is well connected in the cosmetic and consumer products industries and could provide a good overview of current industry trends and developments that might be helpful to me. I promise to be brief and take only a few minutes of her time."*

Secretary   *"All right, Dick; let me see if she will take your call."*

Networker   *"Thank you, Carolyn."*

Although at first this may seem like an impenetrable barrier, you can see how, with a little effort and polite persistence, it can melt away and you can achieve your networking objective. The key words here are "polite persistence." Guard against showing your frustration and remain pleasantly persistent in your efforts to achieve contact with your networking target.

Usually, when an executive takes the position that he or she will not provide job search assistance, the real concern is that he or she will be expected to furnish job leads. Most managers simply don't wish to expose themselves to this possibility and therefore use the secretary as a barrier to prevent such contact. By removing this concern and assuring the secretary that you are only calling for the boss's general counsel and advice (and *not* job leads), you help the secretary clearly see the distinction. At worst, the assistant may first check with the boss to see if he or she is willing to talk, in which event the answer could still be no. However, since you were referred by someone your target contact knows either personally or professionally, a negative response is unlikely.

Example F: The Boss is Too Busy to Take Your Call

Secretary   *"Craig, I'm sorry, but Ms. Swanson is just too busy to take your call."*

Networker   *"I see. Well, I certainly don't want to impose in any way. Perhaps I could call back at a more convenient time. What does Jane's schedule look like over the next couple of weeks. Is there a time that would appear to be convenient? I will only need a few brief minutes of her time, and would very much like to talk with her."*

Secretary *"Well, you might try next Thursday afternoon, late in the day. There is nothing on her schedule at that time and perhaps she may be able to talk with you."*

Networker *"I will plan to try then. Thank you, Jane."*

When a busy schedule is the barrier, remove this obstacle by offering to call back at a more convenient time. If you encounter no further resistance at that point, then try to determine when a convenient time would be for you to place this return call.

When the assistant furnishes you with a suggested time, it is a clear signal that he or she has softened and has taken the first step toward helping you reach the boss. This will help the "call back" go more smoothly since you will be calling at the specific time suggested by the secretary. When making the return call, therefore, it is a good idea to remind the secretary that you are calling back at his or her suggestion.

Example G: My Manager Suggests You Contact Our Employment Department

Secretary *"Mr. Stevens suggests you contact Jan Higgins in our employment department."*

Networker *"Kathy, I certainly appreciate Jack's suggestion. Please tell him that I said thank you. However, I'm not sure that Jan can really help me since I am not looking for a job. What I really need is some insight of some of the current trends and events in food manufacturing that could impact my career transition. Since Jack is a senior operations executive in the food industry, Peter Bryle seemed to feel that he would be an excellent person to speak with on this subject. I would really appreciate the opportunity to speak with him."*

Secretary *"I see. Let me explain this to Mr. Stevens and see if he can take your call."*

Networker *"Thank you, Kathy. I really appreciate your help."*

This objection is somewhat difficult since the administrative assistant has already spoken with his or her boss and it has been suggested that the call be transferred to the employment manager. Now, you are faced with the dilemma of asking the assistant to go back to the well a second time for the purpose of rechecking the boss's decision. However, you have furnished some additional ammunition that should prove helpful. By further clarifying your intent, the boss may relent and agree to grant you the audience you have requested.

We have now dealt with some of the toughest objections you will encounter when attempting to get past the gatekeeper. Armed with the networking strategies and techniques covered in this chapter, and some friendly, polite persistence, you will find that much of this initial resistance usually gives way and you succeed in getting through to your networking contact.

But what about the actual networking call itself? Once you have gotten by the secretary and reached your target contact, what should you expect? What can you do to be sure that your call will be successful? What kind of additional barriers can you expect to encounter, and what should you do to effectively overcome them? These, and related issues, are the topic of the next chapter.

Chapter 8

How to Overcome Key Networking Barriers

There are several common barriers you will encounter while networking. Unless you are fully prepared to deal with these objections effectively at the time they are raised, you will lose the opportunity to exploit your networking contacts and your networking efforts will fall far short of their potential. It is the purpose of this chapter, then, to discuss these various objections and provide you with some suggested approaches and strategies for effectively countering them, thereby making the most of each of your networking opportunities.

"I Don't Have Time to Meet with You"

When you request a personal meeting with a potentially important networking contact and are turned down because the manager doesn't have time to meet with you, it is difficult to know whether or not this objection is valid. The question is whether the networking contact is really too busy or whether he or she is simply using a busy schedule as an excuse for not really wanting to meet with you.

When encountering this particular objection, there is no point in questioning its validity. Simply accept the objection at face value, acknowledge the contact's busy work schedule, and state your willingness to talk with them by phone at a time that is mutually convenient. Here are some sample networking calls that illustrate how this objection can be effectively handled.

Example A

Contact   *"I'm sorry, John; although I would normally be willing to meet with you, my current work schedule simply is not going to allow me to do this. I hope you understand."*

Networker   *"No problem, Barbara. I can appreciate that you have a very busy schedule and a number of demands on your time. Certainly, I don't want to impose. Perhaps, then, we can cover this matter by phone rather than in person. Is this a good time to talk, or would you prefer me to call back at a more convenient time?"*

Contact   *"Actually, I am a bit rushed at the moment."*

Networker   *"Fine, Barbara, when would you suggest I call back?"*

Contact   *"Friday, after 2:00 p.m. might be a good time to try."*

Networker   *"Great! Let me call you back then. I'll look forward to talking with you again on Friday afternoon."*

Example B

Contact   *"I'm sorry, I have an extremely busy schedule and it would be very difficult for me to meet with you at this time."*

Networker   *"That's okay Dave; I can appreciate that you are very busy at this time. In the interest of conserving you time, then, perhaps we can discuss this matter by phone. I promise to take only a few minutes of your time. Is this a convenient time for you?"*

Contact   *"I suppose this is as good a time as ever. How can I help you?"*

"I Don't Know of Any Jobs for You"

Many networking contacts simply assume that you are calling them for job leads. Sometimes this is in spite of the fact that the networker has been very careful to use the indirect approach and has studiously avoided making a direct request for either jobs or job leads. Nonetheless, some contacts will assume this is why you are calling. So, you must be prepared to effectively handle this objection if it is raised during the course of your networking conversation.

Your best strategy is to attempt to neutralize the objection by indicating that this is clearly *not* the reason for your call. Instead, state that the real purpose of your call is to secure the contact's general ideas and advice, rather than specific job leads. Hopefully, this is all it will take to put your networking contact at ease and soon he or she will begin to start talking.

Here are a couple of examples how to successfully deal with this objection.

Example A

Contact   *"Gee, Drew, I don't know of any job openings for an accounting manager."*

Networker   *"That's not a problem, Laura. Actually, I was not expecting you to be aware of a specific job. That's really not why I called. Instead, I was hoping that you might share some general thoughts and ideas concerning my overall job-search strategy. In particular, I would appreciate your overall assessment of the current state of the food industry. What general insights can you share that could impact my job-search strategy?"*

Example B

Contact   *"I'm not sure that I can help you, Linda. I'm just not aware of any opening for research chemists right now."*

Networker   *"Actually, Dave, that's not really why I called. Joan told me that you recently were successful in making your own career transition. I was hoping, as a result, you might have some suggestions about job-hunting strategies. What seemed to work for you? Are there some approaches you would recommend?"*

As you can see, the technique to use to successfully deflect this objection is to take them off the hook by reinforcing that you were not expecting job leads, and then quickly transition the discussion to topics where your contact can "deliver."

"I Don't Think I Can Help You"

This is an objection normally encountered near the beginning of the networking conversation, oftentimes before the networker has had the proper time to frame the networking role and qualify his or her expectations. It usually stems from the fact that many contacts are simply not aware of the many areas in which they can be helpful to the job seeker. Typically, they are thinking more narrowly about their role and how they will furnish job leads—something most are not equipped to deliver.

Successfully countering this objection requires that you properly frame the role of the contact, making your expectations clearly understood. Here is where advance planning of the networking call can have great payoff. You should already have well-established networking objectives that are geared to those areas in which the contact is most likely able to deliver. Simply drawing on these pre-established objectives when framing your networking call expectations, is usually enough to settle the contact down and refocus thinking on those areas where he or she are likely to be most comfortable. The following examples should help you formulate an effective strategy for addressing this objection:

Example A

Contact   *"Don, although I'd like to be of assistance, I'm not sure I can help you."*

Networker   *"Bob, although on the surface this may appear to be the case, there are some areas where I feel your general knowledge and advice could be particularly beneficial to me. For example, Tracy tells me that you are very active in the Marketing Association, and know a lot of marketing executives on both a national and regional basis. Are there specific marketing people whom you know from your professional affiliations that have contacts in the food industry?"*

Example B

Contact   *"Karen, I'm not sure I can really help you."*

Networker   *"Actually, Dick, if you wouldn't mind, there are a couple of areas where I feel I might benefit from your general advice and counsel. For example, I am told by Sheri Williams that you are very knowledgeable about overall trends within the paper industry. I would be particularly interested in any overall observations you could make about current industry trends that might have an impact on my job-search strategy. As an example, what general observations can you make about such things as industry growth trends, new emerging products and markets, key problems faced by the industry, new opportunity areas, and the like? What appear to be the areas for growth and opportunity within the paper industry today?"*

You can see how it is possible to recast the contact's role in the networking discussion to that of a "general advisor." This is a role with which most contacts are very comfortable, and such shift in emphasis should refocus the contact's attention to those areas in which he or she has expertise and can likely deliver.

"You Need to Talk to Our Human Resources Department"

In some cases, as soon as it becomes clear that you are looking for employment, your networking contact may immediately suggest that you contact the Human Resources Department. Such a recommendation is usually tantamount to the "kiss of death." It is extremely rare that such a referral will have positive payoff of any kind. It is important, therefore, that you know how to diplomatically counter this obstacle and encourage a more productive networking conversation.

It has been my experience when a networking contact refers a networker to the human resources or employment function, there has been a breakdown in basic networking communications strategy. Although the networker's intended message is "I need your help," the contact's interpretation is "I need a job." The result is a fast referral to personnel. The following sample networking conversations should give you some ideas on ways to effectively overcome this barrier.

Example A

Contact   *"You need to contact John Dawson, our human resources manager. He handles all matters related to employment. Let me get John's extension for you."*

Networker   *"Yes, I appreciate the referral and will certainly give John a call. Dave, my intent, however, was not to ask you for a job lead or employment application. Instead, I was calling at the suggestion of Karen Freeman to get some general career advice. Karen seemed to feel you would be an excellent person to talk with, in a general sense, about the feasibility of making a career transition to the environmental industry. She felt you would have some excellent insight on this subject. Would you mind taking a few moments to answer a couple of basic questions that I have?"*

Example B

Contact   *"Jane, all employment matters are handled by Sam Dillon in our Corporate Employment Department. If you would like to call back, Sam's direct extension is 445."*

Networker   *"Gee, Melody, I appreciate the referral, but I'm not sure that Sam can help me, since I am not calling about a job at Borton Company. Actually, I was hoping to speak with you personally. In my discussion with Linda Miller, she seemed to feel you would be a good person from whom to get some general advice concerning my career transition strategy. I would really value your personal opinion and was wondering whether you might share some general ideas and advice in a couple of areas. Would this be a good time to talk, or would you prefer me to call back at a more convenient time?"*

Notice how in both of these examples, the networker uses the name of the original referral source to reposition the networking discussion and direct a personal appeal to the networking contact for personal guidance and advice. Use of the referral source's name gently reinforces the sense of social obligation and enhances the probability that the networking contact will respond favorably to your request for personal assistance.

I Have No Suggestions or Ideas for You

Although you will rarely face this specific objection, there are legitimate cases when the networking contact genuinely cannot think of any good suggestions or ideas to share with you. Generally this is symptomatic of individuals who are preoccupied with other matters and are simply not in a creative or reflective state of mind. In such cases, either one of two strategies is recommended as a way of getting the conversation "off dead center":

1. Offer to call back at a more convenient time.
2. Transition your request from a request for advice to a request for the names of networking contacts

Here are some examples of ways to overcome this particular objection.

Example A

Contact   *"I'd really like to help you, Mary, but right now I just simply can't come up with any creative ideas or suggestions with regard to your job search."*

Networker   *"That's okay Keith. Perhaps this is not a good time to be talking. Would there be a time that would be more convenient for you?"*

Example B

Contact   *"I'm afraid I just can't think of any ideas or suggestions for you at this time."*

Networker   *"That's certainly not a problem, Martha. I know if you were to think of something appropriate, you would be happy to share it with me. Perhaps, however, we could shift our focus to another area. As you know, in this tough labor market, job-hunting success is very much dependent upon personal referral and networking. As you think about persons you know in the steel industry through either trade or professional association activities, are there key individual who are well-connected and with whom you feel it would be a good idea to make contact?"*

"I Can't Think of Any Good Contacts for You"

When people through whom you are networking cannot seem to come up with the names of key networking contacts for you, it is usually a sign that they are thinking too narrowly about the kinds of contacts that could prove helpful. Generally, they are focusing on only those people they feel would be in a position to know of actual jobs or job leads. In such cases, it should become your objective to focus their attention on a much broader array of possible networking contacts. The following illustrates some techniques for successfully countering this type of objection:

Example A

Contact   *"Joan, I can't really think of any good contacts for you at the moment."*

Networker   *"Listen, Jerry, perhaps you are thinking too narrowly on my request. I'm not thinking about only those contacts who may be aware of a specific job opening for me. Instead, I am thinking about others who are well connected and seem to know a lot of others in the industry. For example, Jerry, these could include vendors who sell to the industry, people you know through trade or professional association meetings, industry consultants, key educators, or others who are in a position to know a lot of people in the industry. Are there people who fit these categories with whom I should be in contact? I would welcome your thoughts on this."*

Example B

Contact   *"I really can't think of any good contacts for you, Pete. Wish I could help."*

Networker   *"Sometimes it helps to think about categories of contacts. This frequently serves to remind people of key contacts who they would not normally think of. For example, Steve, think about some of the various categories of people within the industry with whom you are in frequent contact. These could include sales representatives, vendors, equipment and chemical manufacturers, raw material suppliers, distribution sources, consultants, educators—anyone who has familiarity with the automotive industry. Are there some key people who fit these categories, with whom I should be in contact?"*

"I'm Not Sure How My Contacts Would Feel About My Giving You Their Name

If you practice good networking techniques, this is an objection that you should seldom, if ever, encounter. However, in the event that you do encounter this barrier, you will need to be equipped to effectively tackle it.

If you don't, you'll surely bring your networking efforts to a screeching halt!

In some cases, your contact will offer to make contact with these referrals personally rather than simply refer you to them. Unfortunately, the world is paved with good intentions, and many of these offers never actually materialize. It is better, in these cases, to attempt to persuade your source that you will deal with these referrals in an appropriate manner. In fact, if your source wishes that their names not be used at all in the referral, you can assure him or her of your willingness to keep the source of the referral confidential.

These examples suggest ways to appropriately address this objection:

Example A

Contact *"Since some of my friends might object, I make it a point of not making personal referrals of this type without first checking with them. If you want, why don't you send your resume to me, and I will glad to speak to them in your behalf."*

Networker *"That's very kind of you. I will send you some copies of my resume in today's mail. When would be a good time to follow up with you to determine the outcome of your discussions?"*

Example B

Contact *"Generally, I have a personal policy of not making unsolicited referrals of this type. I'm never quite sure how my contacts might feel about receiving such calls."*

Networker *"I can appreciate your feelings. Some people are not very diplomatic in the way they handle referrals of this type, and many have a tendency to make a pest of themselves. I can assure you that is not the case here, however. I certainly have no intent of hounding your contacts for a job. That's just not my style. If you prefer, however, I would be glad to protect your identity and to tell your contacts that my referral source is confidential. In this way, there is no possibility that you could be personally compromised."*

"I Don't Take Networking Calls

Although few and far between, there are some individuals who will tell you outright that they simply don't take networking calls. Hidden behind the stated objection is usually one of two reasons for their position:

1. They are concerned that you will ask them for a job or job leads.

2. They are particularly busy and resent the uninvited interruption.

Although this is a fairly difficult objection to deal with, here are a few approaches you might try in an effort to "soften them up."

Example A

Contact *"I'm sorry, Gene, but I don't take networking calls."*

Networker *"I can appreciate that such calls can sometimes be bothersome. I promise to be brief, however, and do not intend to ask you for job leads. I only need some general council and advice,*

*and Barbara Smith felt you might be willing to lend a hand.
Could you spare just a moment or two to answer a few basic
questions?"*

Example B

Contact *"John, I'm sorry, but I've been networked to death, and therefore have a policy of not accepting networking calls."*

Networker *"Gee, I'm sorry to hear that. Did you have a bad experience
somewhere along the line?"*

Contact *"No, not necessarily. I just have a very busy schedule and can't
afford to take calls of this kind."*

Networker *"I see. Well, I certainly don't want to impose in any way. Is
there a time, however, when it might be convenient for us to
talk? I would be glad to call you in the evening, early morning,
or whenever it would be more convenient for you. Is there a time
you could suggest? I promise to take only a few brief minutes of
your time. I would really value your advice and counsel."*

Both of these approaches require a certain degree of persistence,
and also may run a small risk of provoking hostility and outright rejection. However, the old saying—"Nothing ventured, nothing gained"
couldn't be more true here. At worst, your contact will again rebuff your
networking attempt. At best, you may penetrate his or her initial resistance and engage your hesitant professional in fruitful discussion. The
choice is yours!

"I Have No Reason to Help You"

This objection suggests that you are dealing with someone who is just
plain rude and feels no obligation whatsoever to hold to the basic principles of social courtesy when dealing with others. This type of response
suggests that your contact feels absolutely no obligation to respond
whatsoever to your requests for assistance. Fortunately, such encounters
are extremely rare in networking, and you are unlikely to encounter this
kind of uncooperative treatment at all.

In the event that you experience this kind of inappropriate behavior on the part of a networking contact, I suggest that you fight fire with
fire. By adopting an almost equally aggressive stance, sometimes the
contact is taken off guard and you can penetrate the thick outer shell of

resistance and positively impact their behavior. The following strategies may prove effective in dealing with such standoffish individuals:

Example A

Contact   *"Quite frankly, Jeff, I see no reason why I should take time to help you. After all, I don't know you personally, and have no obligation to help you in any way."*

Networker   *"You're absolutely right, Brett, you have no reason to help me. With all of the corporate downsizings, however, you never know when you could be on this side of the equation and be needing my help. Perhaps a few minutes may prove a worthwhile investment on your part. You never know when you're going to need a helping hand. How about it, Brett, can you take a few minutes of your time to lend me a hand?"*

Example B

Contact   *"I don't see any reason why I should take time from a busy schedule to help you. Why are you calling me anyway?"*

Networker   *"I realize that this kind of call can be a pain in the butt. But, unfortunately in this kind of labor market there isn't much choice in the matter but to network. This seems to be the way jobs are found out here. Hopefully, you won't find yourself in this kind of position because, believe me, it's not exactly a piece of cake! Actually, I called you at Barb Johnson's suggestion. She seems to feel that you might me able to help me in some way. Perhaps you can spare a minute or two to share some ideas regarding my job-search strategy. I would appreciate your help."*

Both of these approaches require a fairly high degree of assertiveness. There is also the possibility that you could further alienate the networking contact and be the subject of additional abuse. You need to be fairly thick-skinned when dealing with people of this type, and not take their comments personally. Unfortunately, such reaction to your networking overtures is often typical of their normal social behavior and in no way reflects your social graces or overall networking skills.

We have now dealt with some of the more difficult objections you may encounter during the course of your networking campaign. Hopefully the various strategies offered here will prove helpful to you in successfully fielding these key objections and improving your overall skills and confidence as a networker.

Chapter 9

Developing Winning Networking Strategies

Effective networking doesn't just happen by chance. As you've learned, there are key strategies and techniques that go a long way toward getting the kind of information you need. The purpose of this chapter is to acquaint you with several strategies and techniques that should prove helpful in getting your networking contacts to "open up" and provide you with the kind of information and assistance you require. Becoming familiar with these strategies and learning how they are applied should help you formulate the kinds of questions you need to ask in order to become proficient at the networking process.

The "Career Advice" Strategy

The career advice strategy is a networking strategy that is employed to gather valuable information essential to making a good career decision. It is usually employed early in the job-hunting process while the job seeker is still attempting to determine in what career direction he or she may wish to head. Getting key information of this type, from a knowledgeable source, is critical to formulating specific job-search objectives and providing needed focus to one's job search.

Generally, job seekers need career information and advice at this juncture for one of two primary reasons:

1. In order to reaffirm their current career direction
2. In order to examine possible career alternatives

In both cases, the networking objective is "informational" in nature, and requires the networker ask the right questions of a knowledgeable source.

The first rule in seeking career advice, as part of your networking strategy, is to be sure that you are seeking advice from people who are knowledgeable. This means seeking out people who are already working in the target occupation and industry that you have singled out for career exploration purposes. Talking with people already employed in similar jobs, or who are responsible for hiring for such positions, is the only way to get clear, unclouded insight regarding the qualifications needed for employment and success in your target job.

The second key to career advice networking is to be prepared to ask the kinds of questions essential to helping you make a good career decision. Here are some of the questions you may wish to consider when developing your career advice networking strategy:

Employment Qualifications
- What are the basic qualifications normally required for employment in this type of position?
- Are there certain qualifications normally considered "critical" or "essential"?
- What qualifications are normally considered "preferred" or "highly desirable"?

Ability to Compete
- How competitive is the employment market for this type of position?
- Do you feel my current qualifications will allow me to realistically compete with others for such positions? Why?
- Where do my qualifications fall short, and what suggestions do you have for improvement?

Job Content
- What are the attractive elements of this type of work?
- What are the less desirable aspects of this type of position?

Requirements for Success
- What core skills, traits, and characteristics do you feel are essential for successful performance in this type of work? Why?

- How would you describe the profiles of people who would not be well-suited for this type of work?

Advancement and Growth Opportunities
- What is the typical career track for someone who goes into this kind of work? What kinds of career opportunities can this type of work lead to?
- What do you feel are the future career advancement prospects for people entering this field today?
- If you were giving career advice to your own son or daughter, what would you say about this area?

Referral to Others
- Who are those particularly knowledgeable of this field, who could provide me with further career insight?
- Are there other knowledgeable people you would recommend I talk to who could provide firsthand insight about what it is like to work in this field?

As you can see, these are the essential informational networking questions to ask when making a good career decision. Obviously, there is no point in attempting to compete in a field for which your qualifications are not suited or in considering a career shift into a field that offers little future prospects for growth and advancement. Be careful, then, to ask the right questions and to seek the advice of knowledgeable networking contacts who are intimately familiar with the career field you wish to explore.

The following are examples of how you might approach a networking contact to seek such career advice. Of course, you'll need to tailor your introduction to your specific career area.

Example A

Networker *"Lisa, I am considering the possibility of making a career transition into the field of public affairs. Art Baker explained that you have worked in the public affairs for a number of years, and would be a good person to talk with on this topic. I would value your insight and counsel. Do you have a few minutes to answer a few questions for me?"*

Example B

Networker   *"Jeff, I was referred to you by Barbara Cunningham. Barbara and I are close friends, and she seems to feel you could help me with a basic career decision. I am considering a possible career transition into the field of environmental engineering, and was wondering if you might have a few minutes to share some of your knowledge and insight. Barb tells me that you have been working as an engineering manager in the environmental field for the last 10 years or so."*

Following the introductory statement, you should be prepared to ask your networking contact questions that explore such areas as required by employment qualifications, ability to compete, job content, requirements for success, and the like. Also, don't forget to request the names of additional referrals who can help you with your career decision as well. These same referral sources, by the way, can be quite valuable later on, if you have made the decision to pursue this career change and now need good contacts in the field.

The "Job-Hunting Advice" Strategy

The job hunting advice strategy is a variation of informational networking that is aimed at acquiring key information about job-hunting strategies and techniques that could aid you in your job search. The information the job seeker requests usually falls into one or more of the following categories:

- Resume advice
- Cover letter advice
- Advice on interviewing
- Advice on overall approach to job-hunting
- Recommendations on effective job-hunting sources
- Recommendations on effective job-hunting techniques
- Advice on negotiating strategy and techniques
- Referral to other contacts who are "employment knowledgeable"

If you are going to employ the job-hunting advice strategy successfully, you need to follow these important principles:

1. Make sure you are sincere about your desire for job-hunting advice.

2. Avoid using the job-hunting advice strategy as a ruse for securing other information such as key contacts and job leads.

3. Seek job-hunting advice only from knowledgeable professionals who know the employment field (or who have recently concluded a successful job search in your target field).

Unfortunately, the job-hunting advice strategy is an approach that has been frequently abused by many would-be networkers, and has been responsible for giving employment networking a black eye of sorts. The issue, in this case, seems centered around the matter of sincerity.

It has, unfortunately, been widespread practice among many ill-advised job seekers to use the excuse of "resume review" as a ploy for securing other kinds of valuable networking information such as job leads and important networking contacts. Using this ruse, a networker asks a networking contact to review his or her resume with the pretext that the network is interested in suggested changes that would improve the document's effectiveness. This is frequently used as a trick to get the contact to provide other helpful job-search information, but there is absolutely no intention of using the resume advice provided by the networking contact.

Normally, when employing this ruse, the networker will use a statement such as the following:

> *"Bill, I am in the process of making a career move and would appreciate if you would be willing to look over my resume. I would value any changes that you would recommend that might improve the impact and effectiveness of this document."*

However, the real intent is something other than resume review and the networker is only using this tactic to direct the conversation into more meaningful areas.

The problem with this approach is not simply the insincerity with which it is delivered, but also that it has become severely "shop worn." It has been so overused that most seasoned managers and employment professionals immediately recognize it for what it really is. The impressions left with the seasoned networking contact are clearly less then favorable and positive. Today, such insincerity is readily transparent to the experienced networking contact, and you are strongly advised, therefore, to avoid using this tactic. Instead, make sure if you are using the job-hunting advice strategy as part of your networking repertoire, that you do so with sincerity and purpose. Ask only for that information that you need and intend to use.

The other key to effective use of the job-hunting advice strategy is to choose only "employment knowledgeable" professionals to interview. There are a lot of well-intentioned, would-be employment "experts" out there who are more than willing to offer free advice only for the asking. The only problem can be that the information and advice you get in return can be inappropriate and lead to a serious misdirection of your job-search effort.

Generally, when using the job hunting advice strategy as part of your networking arsenal, it's best advised to seek the expert guidance of experienced, knowledgeable, employment professionals (or line managers with heavy employment experience) when seeking advice on:

- Your resume
- Cover letters
- The interviewing process
- Overall job-hunting strategy
- Negotiating strategy and techniques

On the other hand, people with recent job-hunting experience might be helpful in providing you with advice in the following areas:

- Recommendations on effective job-hunting sources
- Recommendations on effective job-hunting techniques
- Referral to others who are employment knowledgeable

The point is, choose your sources wisely when seeking job-hunting advice. Be sure that the person you target for such advise is the "best qualified" to provide valid information in the area you wish to explore.

The following sample introductions provide you with a sense of the job-hunting advice networking strategy. You can use them to tailor your own introductions for networking purposes.

Example A: Employment Professional

"Mike, your name was given to me by Joan Lawson as a very knowledgeable employment professional. Joan and I have worked together in the accounting department of Wilson Company for a number of years. She seems to feel that you would be an excellent person to speak with concerning some general questions I have on my job-search strategy. Is this a good time for you to talk?"

Example B: Employment Professional

"Carolyn, I am calling you at the suggestion of Wilma Davidson. Wilma and I were classmates at Penn State University and have stayed in touch over the years. In view of your extensive employment experience in the beverage industry, she seems to feel you would be an excellent person to talk with for the purpose of getting sound resume advice. Is this a convenient time for you?"

Example A: Person with Recent Job-Search Experience

"Bob, during a recent conversation with John Applebee, he mentioned that you had recently been in the employment market and were successful in securing a position as marketing manager with the Dow Chemical's Specialty Chemicals Division. Since I am looking for a similar position in the chemical industry, John feels you might be in a good position to offer some job-hunting advice. Bob, were there any sources or approaches that you used in your job search that proved particularly effective? What suggestions might you have for me?"

Example B: Person with Recent Job-Search Experience

"Mary, I'm calling you at the suggestion of Bill Johnson. Bill and I know one another from church, where we have served on the finance committee together for the last few years. I understand from Bill that you recently concluded a successful job search for a position as loan officer in the commercial banking field. During my discussion with Bill he suggested that I give you a call since I am looking for a position in the commercial banking field as well. He thought, perhaps, you might pass along some advice that could be helpful to me in my job search. I would certainly appreciate that. Is this a good time for you to talk?"

The "Key Information" Strategy

The term key information strategy, is normally applied to describe the networking strategy used to secure important information about your target industry or target companies that might prove particularly helpful to your job search. Examples of key information that fits this networking category include:

- Current or planned target company expansions
- Target company contractions or downsizing
- Key shifts in corporate strategy
- Key issues or problems faced by target company
- Growth plans and strategies
- New products and markets
- Major shifts in organizational culture
- Restructuring
- Key personnel moves (resignations, retirements, promotions, new hires, deaths)
- Names and titles of target executives

All of these above areas have possible job-search implications and are therefore key areas for exploration when employing the key information networking strategy. Major shifts or changes in organizational strategy and structure often give rise to new employment opportunities that have not become known to the general public and are still in the realm of the hidden job market. You need to use your networking skills, therefore, to stay in touch with what is happening at your target companies so you can ferret out opportunities for employment as they develop, before they become formalized and communicated to the external or public job market.

The purpose of the key information networking strategy, then, is to keep you abreast of these changes as they occur. In this way you greatly improve your employment chances by allowing you to network to new, emerging opportunities as they develop. Such timely networking has the potential to virtually eliminate employment competition if you get to the hiring source early enough in the process.

As part of your key information networking strategy it is important, whenever possible, that you cultivate close networking contacts in each of your key target companies early in your job search. Such people, if properly cultivated, can become your key internal "watch dog," keeping an eye out for major shifts or changes that could have possible job-search ramifications. Developing such internal watch dogs requires some careful networking and cultivation on your part, but it can prove well worth the effort if you are successful at establishing the right kind of relationship.

Generally, this strategy works best when you already have an existing relationship within the target company. It is often possible, however, to cultivate new networking relationships that are willing to keep you abreast of major changes, provided you stay in touch with them on a periodic basis and continually nurture the relationship. Individuals who comprise the most likely targets for effective use of the key information networking strategy normally fall into the following categories:

- People employed in target industry
- Vendors and suppliers to your target industry
- Target industry consultants
- Stock analysts who specialize in your target industry
- Officers of your target industry trade associations (national and regional)
- Key company representatives to trade associations
- Publishers of your target industry publications
- Educators with target industry specialization
- Past employees of target industry companies

All of these people have the potential to hear about key industry information that could prove vital to your job search as a result of their continuous contact and close working relationships within the industry. The general industry grapevine can be a powerful information source for employment networking purposes if you make effective use of your network contacts to stay fully plugged into industry changes as they actually occur.

The following are some examples of how this important strategy can be used to your advantage when networking through target industry contacts:

Example A

"Jim, as a sales representative who is in daily contact with numerous procurement professionals in the cosmetics industry, I am sure you occasionally become aware of major industry and company changes before they become knowledge to the general public. What major industry changes have you observed that might suggest opportunities for someone with a strong procurement management background? Are you aware, for example, of any major restructuring or personnel changes in the procurement area anywhere in the industry?"

Example B

"Judy, Dexter Corporation is one of the firms that I have targeted as part of my job-search strategy. What are some of the major shifts and changes in organizational structure and/or strategy that could impact the operations function there at the company? Also, what appear to be some of the major problems and/or issues with which they are currently occupied?"

Example C

"Harry, what can you tell me about some of the major strategic shifts at Dolan Company that are part of the company's growth strategy? Are there any anticipated expansions of the company's product line or other specific growth strategies on which the company appears particularly focused at this time?"

The "Informational Meeting" Strategy

One of the most effective employment networking strategies is the informational meeting strategy. Meeting face to face with a networking contact is known to be far more effective than simply having a telephone discussion. The chemistry and personal rapport developed between the networker and the networking contact during such meetings appear to create a stronger bond between the two and increased commitment, on the part of the contact, toward helping the networker.

The basis for setting up these face-to-face meetings is known as the informational meeting strategy. When using this strategy, the networker simply requests a meeting with the networking contact on the basis of wanting to use this opportunity to secure information important to the success of his or her job search.

When employing this strategy, there is a whole host of information that the networker can attempt to acquire from the networking contact:

- Career advice
- Job search advice
- Industry information
- Company information
- Names of key networking contacts

The following are examples of how you might employ the informational meeting strategy as an effective networking tool.

Example A

> *"Wanda, Mike English suggested that I give you a call. Mike and I are neighbors, and he was telling me that you are very active on the Board of Directors of the Marketing Council. Since I am currently seeking a position in marketing management, Mike seems to feel that you would be an excellent sounding board for my job-search strategy. I would really value your counsel and advice. Would it be possible for us to get together for an hour or so, sometime in the next couple of weeks?"*

Example B

> *"Walter, this is Sandra Willingston calling. In a conversation with Beverly Dodds the other evening, she mentioned that you are a certified financial planner and suggested that I give you a call. I am considering a career change from corporate finance to financial planning, and Beverly thought you might be willing to meet with me to share some of your insights concerning the financial planning field. I would really appreciate your advice on this subject. Would it be possible for us to get together sometime during the next few weeks?"*

When requesting an informational meeting, it is usually best to position your request as a need for information and/or advice. As you know, requests for more "direct" information, such as key contacts or job leads, are best reserved for discussion during the meeting itself. Positioning job leads as the key reason for desiring a face-to-face meeting may be simply "too direct" and turn some networking contacts off. Why push your luck? You will get much further by telling your contact that you would appreciate his or her counsel and advice.

The "Who Do You Know That . . ." Strategy

The "who do you know that . . ." strategy is a networking strategy designed to help you identify key networking contacts who could be particularly helpful in some aspect of your job search. It is primarily intended to identify people who are expert in a given area or who have special knowledge of one of your target companies.

Since this is a fairly direct strategy, you should probably reserve it for later in your networking discussion, when you feel you have established a reasonable level of personal rapport with your networking contact. If used properly, it is a very effective technique for getting the names of important networking contacts who could be particularly helpful to you in your job search. This networking strategy can be used to identify key contacts fitting any one of the following categories:

- Target executives
- Employees of target companies
- People knowledgeable of target industry and/or target companies
- Employment experts

Here are some examples of how this strategy can be used to secure the names of vital contacts in these categories.

Example A

> *"Carol, whom do you know at the Wallace Company that probably knows Skip Baker, Wallace's vice president of marketing? If possible, I would like to arrange for an introduction to Skip."*

Example B

> *"Lan, whom do you know at the Wharton Company that works in either accounting or finance, and would be a good person to talk with?"*

Example C

> *"Susan, whom do you know, that is knowledgeable and well connected in the electronics field? Is there anyone who you believe it would be good for me to talk with?"*

Example D

> *"John, whom do you know that is an employment expert and might be a good person from whom to get resume and job-hunting advice? Is there anyone you can recommend?"*

When using this particular strategy it is very important to wait until you are comfortable that you have established a fairly friendly and open relationship with your networking contact. Premature use of this strategy can cause some contacts to feel nervous, so use this approach only when it is evident that you have been successful in establishing a fairly relaxed relationship.

The "Key Personnel Moves" Strategy

The "key personnel moves" strategy is a networking approach designed to help your networking contact remember possible job leads through the process of association. By questioning your networking contact about key personnel moves in your target industry, you hope to identify possible job opportunities that could have been created as a result of such moves.

Key personnel moves fit the following general categories:

- Promotions
- Transfers
- New hires
- Retirements
- Resignations
- Involuntary terminations
- Extended medical leaves (long-term disabilities)
- Deaths

When using this networking strategy, don't just inquire as to whether your networking contact is aware of such personnel moves, but also mention a few of the above categories in an effort to trigger your contact's memory. By mentioning these categories you can sometimes "pop" additional information through the process of association. The following examples illustrate the use of the key personnel moves networking strategy:

Example A

"Debbie, as you know, I am currently seeking a position in project engineering management in the power industry. Are you aware of any key personnel moves in the power industry that might give rise to a suitable opportunity for me? For example, recent promotions, resignations, retirements, new hires, involuntary separations, and the like?"

Example B

"As you know, Jim, sometimes key personnel moves can lead to the creation of new employment opportunities. Can you think of any key personnel changes that have recently occurred in the industry that I might want to look into? For example, resignations, retirements, promotions, illnesses, or new hires."

In general, it is not considered good taste to bring up disabilities or deaths in the course of networking when you are attempting to use the key personnel moves strategy as a vehicle for identifying possible employment opportunities. As you read personnel announcements in industry-related publications, however, you may want to stay alert to obituaries. As crass as it may sound, they suggest a need for identification of someone to fill the position that has been vacated by the deceased.

The "Key Contacts" Strategy

As the title suggests, this strategy is used to secure the names of key contacts in both your target industry and target companies. It is generally designed to identify people who are exceptionally well connected and have a large volume of valuable contacts in the industry you have targeted as your job-search objective.

In applying this strategy, simply ask your networking contact for the names of people who are well connected in the target industry. Using some further definition of what well connected means can sometimes prompt your networking contact to come up with the names of additional valuable contacts. The examples that follow illustrate how to effectively utilize this networking strategy:

Example A

> *"George, as you know, I'm trying to penetrate the steel indus-try as my primary industry target. Who do you know that is well connected and appears to have a number of contacts in the steel industry? Are there people you can think of with whom I should probably be in contact?"*

Example B

> *"Betsy, are there key contacts in the pharmaceutical industry with whom it is helpful to network? In particular, are there peo-ple who come to mind whom you believe to be well connected and appear to know a number of others within the industry?"*

The "Industry Trends and Happenings" Strategy

This is a good general strategy that is usually best positioned near the beginning of the networking discussion. It is a fairly nonthreatening strategy designed to get the networking contact comfortable and serves as a very effective social warm-up technique. It also sometimes yields some valuable information that can prove quite helpful to your overall job-search strategy.

Here are some examples of how this particular strategy can be em-ployed:

Example A

> *"Sandra Jones tells me that you are particularly knowledge-able about the state of the banking industry, and would be a good person to talk with for an overview of what is currently happening in the industry. Dave, what are some of the current trends and happenings within the banking industry that, in your judgment, might have an impact on my current job search?"*

Example B

> *"As a key trade association officer, I am sure that you have a unique understanding and overview of the industry that few others have. Beth, what observations can you make about some of the current industry trends and specific happenings that might have an impact on my job-search strategy. And, as a result, what specific recommendations do you have for me?"*

The "Professional Trends and Happenings" Strategy

This networking strategy is the close cousin of the industry trends and happenings strategy. The difference is that it is a specific strategy used to gain insight into key professional trends and events that could have an impact on your approach to job hunting. Instead of industry contacts, this strategy is aimed at getting important information from fellow professionals who specialize in your occupational field. These are the people whom you have met at professional society meetings and who are typically your professional counterparts in other organizations.

In many cases, the people whom you choose as the subjects for this networking approach should be professionals whom you know to be well connected and heavily networked with others in your profession. It is an ideal strategy to use with both the regional and national officers of your professional association. These individuals, in particular, are usually well aware of current trends and events within your occupational field.

The following examples show how to use this strategy to gain valuable job-search advice from these target individuals:

Example A

"As regional vice-president of the American Statistical Association, what information can you share with me about current trends and happenings in our profession that might impact my current job-search strategy? Are there specific recommendations that you can make?"

Example B

"Keith, from you perspective, what current trends and happenings in the field of engineering do you feel might have greatest impact on my current job search? What do you feel it would be helpful for me to know?"

The "Laundry List" Strategy

The laundry list strategy is, by far, one of the most effective networking strategies I have seen to help the networker secure the names of key networking contacts, as it makes extensive use of association as a tool to help networking contacts surface the names of key contacts they would not otherwise remember. When used effectively, this technique alone can account for a fourfold increase in networking results.

Since employment networking accounts for some 68 percent of

employment results, any technique that can increase a person's networking effectiveness by a factor of four can significantly impact job-search time. Logic suggests that securing, on average, four times the networking referrals per call has the potential to reduce job-search time by 75 percent or better. This is a good reason to become particularly proficient in the use of this important networking strategy.

The laundry list is a technique used in conjunction with the networker's request for key networking contacts within the target industry. In using this technique, the networker not only asks the current contact for the names of additional people for networking purposes, but also combines this request with a "laundry list" of the categories or kinds of contacts that could prove particularly helpful. Examples of such categories include the following:

- Sales representatives
- Vendors
- Suppliers
- Consultants
- Contractors
- Educators
- Trade association officers (local and national)
- Key industry leaders

Providing your networking contact with such a laundry list of contact categories provides two very important advantages:

1. The recitation of these categories allows the networking contact more time to think of additional names.
2. Through the process of association, the listing of categories usually serves as an excellent stimulus to assist your contact in recalling several additional contact names that he or she would not otherwise have remembered.

To facilitate use of this strategy, keep a three-by-five- inch index card handy with a laundry list of these categories written on it. The following illustrations show how this technique can be effectively used to your networking advantage.

Example A

"Who are some of the people you can think of that are well-connected and know a lot of others in the industry? For example, sales representative, vendors and suppliers, consultants, contractors, association officers, or others you know and feel would be good for me to contact?"

Example B

"Chris, as you think about key contacts you know within the industry, who are some of the people you know whom you believe to have an extensive network—those who have a lot of industry contacts? For example, these might include such individuals as sales representatives, key industry leaders, trade association officers, professional associates, consultants, educators, or others with significant industry contacts."

Hopefully this chapter has armed you with some good strategies to get the most out of your networking contacts. Certainly, it should provide you with the ammunition needed to open your contacts up and get them talking about the elements that are important to the success of your job search. Using these techniques to keep the pipeline full of fresh networking contacts is, of course, the very lifeline to keeping the employment process alive and well. It is the basis for continual renewal and revitalization of your overall job-hunting effort.

Now shift your focus away from the subject of specific networking strategies and turn your attention and energy to the topic of networking efficiency.

Chapter 10

Key Networking Tricks and Shortcuts

With employment networking playing such a critical role in the overall job-hunting campaign, it is important that you not only become skilled in the use of basic networking strategies and techniques but that you look for ways to become more efficient in carrying out the overall networking process. It stands to reason that anything that can be done to shorten the networking process should have the potential to shorten the overall job search as well. Simply stated, the more efficient you are at networking, the shorter your job search will be. Therefore, this chapter, explores ways to shortcut the employment networking process with the goal of helping you cut unnecessary time off of your job-hunting effort and return to the ranks of the "happily employed" at an early date.

The Long, Long Chain Concept
One of the biggest problems with conventional networking approaches is what I call the "long, long chain concept." Part of the greatest frustration with the networking process is simply the enormous number of calls that must be made to achieve any measurable results. People must travel a long, long way down the chain of networking contacts before they eventually network to their target executives and uncover a bonafide job opportunity.

In fact, it is estimated that most job opportunities are not uncovered until the networker has reached the fifth or sixth level (or further) of the networking chain. This normally translates into hundreds of calls in order to land a single bonafide interview. No wonder most job seekers find the networking process so very frustrating (and depressing). One must endure an incredible amount of rejection before getting that single positive nod.

Unfortunately, conventional networking theory has accepted this frustration as a given, and has done little to look for ways to shortcut the process. It accepts the premise that "this is just the way it is," and drops the issue there. But what about the pain that people must endure? Can't something be done to help them?

The Target Executive

At this point you're probably asking yourself, "If the whole purpose of networking is to gain access to target executives who can hire me, then, is it absolutely necessary to make all of these hundreds of networking calls reach them?" Good question! I believe the answer is no! There must be some ways to shortcut the process and enable you to access these individuals much sooner. If you can do this, it should stand to reason, that you should be able to cut considerable time off of the job-hunting process, and find employment sooner (a pleasant thought) Okay, then, how about it? What are some of the techniques that can be used to accomplish this?

Professional and Trade Associations

Your greatest ally in shortcutting the networking process can be either professional or trade association contacts. Chapter 4 went to great lengths to describe how to use professional and trade associations to research and identify target companies and executives. Well, the same research methodology can also be used as the basis for shortcutting the networking process as well. Here's how it works.

As you know, the key element that makes the networking process work is the sense of social or professional obligation that is felt when you are referred to a networking contact by someone he or she knows. Although it is slightly different, there is also a certain level of fraternal or professional obligation that goes along with being a member of a professional or trade association. The term "fraternal obligation" is more descriptive of the professional association relationship, while the term "professional obligation" is more precisely attached to the trade association relationship.

Nonetheless, such obligation comes with the territory. If you are a member of a professional or trade association, and are approached by a fellow member for advice or help, it is expected that you respond positively and appropriately. To do otherwise is a violation of the unwritten professional bonds that hold such organizations together—a professional affront, so to speak. Put differently, it is fair game to call upon fellow association members for "advice and counsel." That's what they are there for, isn't it!?

Networking Through Association Members

How do you network through association members and end up with introductions to your target executives? Or better yet, is there a way of networking directly to these executives without the necessity of all those phone calls? The answer to both questions is yes, although as you will see, I believe the idea of first networking through others in the organization is clearly the way to go. Before you can begin networking, there are a couple of preliminary steps that need to be taken:

1. Research and identify your target companies (See Chapter 4, pages 49 to 53).
2. Research and identify your target executives (See Chapter 4, pages 54 to 56).
3. Research and join key professional associations (secure membership directory).
4. Research and join key trade association (secure membership directory).
5. Research and identify functional peers in target organizations.

The research methods used for accomplishing the above steps are fully described in chapter 4, so if you have not already read chapter 4, let me suggest that you consider doing so. The net result of the above research will be the preparation of an extensive list of key contacts who work directly in the target functional areas and companies that you have selected for purposes of your job search. This includes both target executives as well as peer level persons who work in the target functions. Once this listing is complete and you have prepared call sheets on each person (see chapter 5), you are ready to begin making networking calls.

When making these networking calls, begin by first calling those individuals who work directly for your target executives. After you have talked with these people, then give the target executive a call as well.

The reason for this calling sequence is simple. By first calling the subordinates, you have the opportunity to systematically collect "intelligence" about the target executive and his or her function. Learning about critical items such as strategic objectives and key issues faced by the group, for example, in advance of your networking call to the target executive, can provide you with a very real strategic advantage, when it comes time to make that all-important call. Besides, you may be able to get one of the lower-level managers to agree to make the introduction, especially if it appears that you could offer some possible solutions to some of the business issues with which the group is wrestling.

By networking directly into the target group you can most likely do away with the numerous additional calls required by conventional networking methods and arrive at the same point far more quickly. It is conservatively estimated that such "direct" calling can cut the number of required networking calls by 50 percent or better! Not a bad objective, is it?

The Association Networking Approach

When making calls to association members, the overall tactics and techniques are similar to those used in conventional networking. The only basic difference is the initial introduction. Here, instead of using the name of your referral source to create the sense of obligation to respond, you substitute your association membership as the basis for creating this feeling of obligation. The following two examples illustrate how such an introduction might be made:

Example A

Networker   *"Good morning Beth, this is Bob Duncan calling. How are you this morning?"*

Contact   *"Just fine, Bob, how are you?"*

Networker   *"Just great, Beth, thank you. Beth, this morning I was going through my Accounting Association membership roster and came across your name. So, I decided to give you a call. Actually, I'm in the process of a career transition and thought, as a fellow member of the Accounting Association, you might be in a position to offer some advice and ideas. Is this a good time for you to talk?"*

Example B

Networker   *"Hello, George, this is Mike Houston calling. I'm a fellow member of the Information Services Association, and noticed that you are also a member. Have you been a member for long?"*

Contact   *"Yes, I've belonged to the Association for close to 10 years now, and usually get to most annual meetings."*

Networker   *"Yes, I've been to quite a few of the annual meetings myself. In fact, I thought the Chicago meeting back in October was one of the better ones I've attended so far. Were you there?"*

Contact   *"No, unfortunately, my work schedule just wouldn't permit it, but I hope to get to the meeting in Atlanta this fall."*

Networker   *"Me too! Listen, George, the reason I am calling is to get a little professional advice, and I was wondering if you could give me a hand."*

Contact   *"I'll try. What kind of advice do you need?"*

Networker   *"Actually, George, I'm in the process of a career transition, and am calling you for some general advice and ideas concerning my job-search strategy. I would really appreciate your counsel."*

Contact   *"Great! What can I do for you?"*

(*Note:* Continue with conventional networking approaches as described in previous chapters).

As you can see from these above examples, this approach is very similar to traditional networking except that the "association relationship" is simply substituted in the place of the "personal referral." If positioned properly, the association relationship and professional courtesy that goes along with it can be a pretty powerful force in compelling networking contacts to be supportive of your request for assistance. In many cases, it can be as powerful as the personal referral technique.

Probing for Target Company Information

Once you have followed a typical networking agenda and received both advice and the names of key contacts, it is time to direct the conversation to the target company itself. In many cases this transition will happen naturally, and it won't be necessary to use the following approach. If not, however, the following dialogue is a way to segue into such discussion:

Example A

> *"Dave, quite frankly, one of the companies that I had targeted for my job search is the Baxter Company. Can you tell me what is happening in the Accounting Department at Baxter these days? One of my target contacts is Bill Ross [Baxter's corporate controller], and I thought it might be helpful to get some inside information about what is happening there prior to giving Bill a call. What can you tell me that might be helpful?"*

Example B

> *"Donna, I am also interested in employment opportunities there at Dawson Company, and am planning to give Dwayne Dixon [your target executive] a call. Can you provide me with any insight about what is happening in the Marketing Department there? What can you tell me about your marketing strategy as well as some of the key issues that Dwayne is currently wrestling with? Is there anything that you can share with me that can provide me with some insight?"*

Obviously, the above strategies are fairly assertive and are not totally without risk. But why not give this line of questioning a shot? You have everything to gain and nothing to lose at this point!

In an estimated 70 percent of the cases or better, your networking contact will begin to open up with you and share key information that will be beneficial to you in preparing a strategy for calling the boss. In another 30 percent, they will back off somewhat and politely explain that they are simply not at liberty to discuss department or company business strategy. In such case, you simply acknowledge the wisdom of such policy and thank them for their time and help.

"Cold Calling" the Target Executive

Wherever possible, it is advisable to network to the target executive through someone he or she knows. As this normally has a much greater success rate. When all else fails, however, it's time to "cold call." This is perhaps the most difficult of all networking calls to make, especially if you have had no prior training in cold call networking techniques.

Whenever possible, use the professional or trade association membership approach as the basis for your introduction. Once the introduction is complete (establishing the membership connection), you will want to follow standard networking call protocol (see chapter 5 for specifics). Other than the fact that this is one of your target executives, there is really nothing different between a cold call and a standard networking call.

When it is not possible to make use of the professional or trade association membership connection as the basis for your introduction to the target executive, things are going to get a lot tougher. In these cases, the key element that holds networking together and makes it work—the sense of professional obligation to respond—is missing. You cannot rely upon the professional or personal kinship that is the basis for the more privileged relationship that comes from membership in the same organization, so your relationship, without specific referral names is relegated to the status of "complete stranger."

However, there are some good networking techniques you can use to "level the landscape" a bit and put yourself in a more leveraged position than that of a stranger. The following are some examples of cold call approaches that might be used to introduce yourself to a target executive, without benefit of a common business or personal connection.

Example A

Networker   *"Bill, this is Karlene Saunders calling. I am the corporate manager of public affairs with Diamond State Corporation in Wilmington, Delaware. How are you this morning?"*

Contact   *"Quite well, Karlene, and how are you doing?"*

Networker   *"Very well, thank you. Bill, I am calling you on a professional confidential basis and would very much appreciate your advice on a personal matter. Is this a convenient time for you?"*

Contact   *"Sure, Karlene, how can I help you?"*

Networker   *"I am in the process of a career transition, and would really appreciate some general advice and ideas concerning my job search strategy."*

(*Note:* Continue with conventional indirect approach to networking.)

Example B

Networker   *"Hello, Rebecca, this is Dane Edwards calling. How are you this afternoon?"*

Contact   *"Just fine, Dane. How can I help you?"*

Networker   *"Rebecca, I have been Director of Manufacturing of Wellco Corporation for the last five years, and am now in the process of a career transition. As a professional associate in the manufacturing field, I felt you would be a good person to call for some general thoughts and ideas concerning my job search. I would really appreciate your support. Is this a good time to talk?"*

(*Note:* Continue with conventional networking approach).

Example C

Networker   *"Good morning, Linda. This is Gordon Hilliard calling. How are you this morning?"*

Contact   *"Very well, Linda, thank you. And how are you?"*

Networker   *"I'm doing well, thank you."*

Contact   *"How may I help you, Gordon?"*

Networker   *"Although we've not met Linda, I've heard your name mentioned from time to time among some of my professional accounting friends here in the Philadelphia area. I've been working as tax manager with Price Waterhouse in their Philadelphia office for the last few years. Linda, rather than beat around the bush, I'll get right to the point of my call. I have decided to leave Price Waterhouse, and am calling you for some general advice and ideas concerning my career transition. I would appreciate if you could take a few moments to talk with me. Is this a good time for you to talk?"*

These examples reveal the use of what I call the "collegial approach" to networking. When using this approach, the networker simply introduces him-or herself as a "professional colleague" in an effort to establish a sense of professional peer relationship. Such introduction tends to put the relationship on a more equal footing and again tugs at the contact's sense of obligation to respond appropriately to requests for assistance from a "fellow professional."

Despite lack of formal membership in a specific association, professionals generally perceive themselves to be a part of a higher calling by virtue of their commitment to their chosen occupational profession. Thus, they see themselves as "human resource professionals," "accounting professionals," "marketing professionals," "supply management professionals," and the like. There is an informal common bond (in other words, the profession) that holds these groups together in a universal fraternal relationship of sorts. There is also an unwritten code of behavior among professionals that requires them to treat one another with mutual respect and an expectation that, when asked, they will help their colleagues.

When cold calling, then, it is important to establish this sense of collegial relationship through the way in which you position your introduction to the networking contact. As seen in the preceding examples, quickly referencing your current (or past) position and company early in the conversation can effectively accomplish this. Using words such as "professional associate," "fellow professional," and the like can also achieve the desired result.

Once the introduction has been made and the professional relationship established, however, continue to use the conventional networking approach (as detailed in chapter 5). Start by asking for general ideas, advice, and information,—using the indirect rather than the direct approach.

Although this kind of cold calling requires some assertiveness on your part, if done professionally, you may discover that it is a lot easier than you think. When making such calls, think of yourself as a professional colleague rather than someone who is looking for a job. Psychologically this will boost your confidence and help you to feel you are on equal footing with those you are contacting. This sense of parity (and confidence) will likely be picked up by your contact, and it will help to reinforce the feelings of fraternal belonging and equality that are at the very heart of all professional relationships.

One final note. Although cold calling can be quite effective and time-saving, wherever possible, you should first try to network your way to your target executives. Professional or personal introductions to these individuals is clearly known to be more effective than making a cold call: there is simply a stronger sense of obligation to respond when such referrals serve as the basis for introductions to these executives.

The "Key Problems" Strategy

There have been a number of articles written on the topic of how to turn a networking conversation with a target executive into a job interview. Most of these center around the idea of selling yourself as someone who can help that executive solve key problems.

This is why it's a good idea to first talk with subordinates prior to contacting your target executive. In this way you have the opportunity to gain some internal intelligence about some of the key problems currently facing this executive. If you know how to solve these problems, or if you have actually been successful in solving similar problems in the past, you should shift the conversation in this direction. By sharing some basic ideas you may quickly find yourself with an invitation to get together for the purpose of discussing the matter further. If this is a particularly knotty problem and you know the answer, you may also eventually find yourself the proud recipient of an employment offer (or consulting assignment).

By using this problem-solving technique, I have seen numerous networks offered consulting assignments by employers. I have also witnessed several cases where these temporary assignments have eventually led to permanent employment, based upon the quality of the work performed during the consulting engagement. If you are wondering how to introduce the problem-solving approach during the course of the networking call, here are some suggestions:

Example A

"Lori, during an earlier networking call with Bill Johnson in your department, he told me about the problem you are having with the XYZ. I had similar problems while at Gilmar Corporation, and have a couple of suggestions you might want to consider."

Example B

"By the way Bill, when I was talking earlier with Debbie Drake, she mentioned the challenge you are faced with in needing to downsize the corporate staff. It's always difficult to decide where to make cuts, especially when there seems to already be more than enough work to go around. If you don't mind the suggestion, you might want to take a re-engineering approach by looking at work redesign from the standpoint of

*value adding versus transactional work, with a view toward
outsourcing the work that is transactional in nature. I led such
an effort at Whidell Corporation, and we were able to cut our
corporate staff by better than 50 percent and reduced operat-
ing costs by almost $20 million in a single year. If it would be
helpful I would be glad to meet and share some of our experiences with you. Perhaps it may provide some insight to a rather
difficult problem."*

The logic behind this particular strategy is simple. Jobs exist because problems exist. If companies had no problems, there would be no
need to hire anyone. So, where there are problems, there are also potential job opportunities. Don't ignore these natural opportunities to create
a position for yourself by being the solution to some manager's problem.

If you think all of this is "farfetched," just remember one thing:
Mark Granovetter, the Harvard sociologist, proved that some 43.5 percent of all jobs that are found through networking are "newly created,"
and did not exist prior to the networking call. Since his study further
showed that some 74.5 percent of all jobs are found through networking,
this means that a full 32 percent of all jobs are not only filled through
networking, but also represent newly created positions arising from the
networking contact! Do you still believe that the key problems networking strategy won't work? I certainly hope not! There appears to be strong
evidence to the contrary.

By now you're probably convinced it isn't necessary to make all
those telephone calls as suggested in the conventional approach to employment networking. Instead, with some good advance research,
proper planning, and thorough practice of the networking techniques
suggested in this chapter, it may be quite possible to cut as much as 50
percent to 75 percent (or more) off networking time. Since networking
plays such a key role in job-search success, this increased job-hunting
efficiency has the potential to cut several unnecessary and unwanted
months off the average job search. This is an objective that is well worth
pursuing!

Happy networking!

Index